IMAGES
of America

LAURENS COUNTY

STEAM ENGINE. The railroad provided a means of transportation for families and also supplied citizens with products and goods from other areas. Connecting the towns and communities of Laurens County, the railroad played an important part in the growth of the area. Steam engines sent billowing puffs of black smoke into the air and created a sense of fascination in residents. (Courtesy James L. Cooper Jr. Collection.)

IMAGES
of America

LAURENS COUNTY

Libby Coats Rhodes and Carol McMahan Chambers

ARCADIA
PUBLISHING

Published by Arcadia Publishing
Charleston, South Carolina

Library of Congress Catalog Card Number: 2001087781

For all general information contact Arcadia Publishing at:
Telephone 843-853-2070
Fax 843-853-0044
E-Mail sales@arcadiapublishing.com
For customer service and orders:
Toll-Free 1-888-313-2665

Visit us on the Internet at www.arcadiapublishing.com

This book is affectionately dedicated to our children,
Mason and Johnson Motes, Nelson and Noah Chambers, and Tara Brown,
with a sincere hope that they will forever study and preserve the history of Laurens County.

LAURENS COUNTY COURTHOUSE. The Laurens County Courthouse is an example of Greek Revival architecture in rural South Carolina. The central portion was constructed in 1837–1838 and is the focal point of the Laurens town square. (Courtesy Laurens County Library.)

CONTENTS

TEAM OF MULES. Mules, such as the matched white pair seen here, were used for farming and transportation by Laurens County farmers. Even into the 1940s, it was common to witness mule-drawn wagons traveling down rural dirt roads and leaving a cloud of dust behind them. The size of a farm was measured by the number of mules in the barn. (Courtesy James L. Cooper Jr. Collection.)

COTTON PICKERS. Fields of snow-white cotton were once a common sight in rural Laurens County. The cotton was picked by hand and weighed at the end of the workday; workers were paid according to the number of pounds picked. Cotton fields and pickers dotted the landscape well into the 1950s. (Courtesy James L. Cooper Jr. Collection.)

INTRODUCTION

On March 12, 1785, Laurens became one of six South Carolina counties created from the Ninety Six district. Located in the piedmont region of upper Carolina, the county was divided into nine townships: Laurens, Dials, Waterloo, Sullivan, Scuffletown, Hunter, Cross Hill, Jacks, and Youngs. The county derived its name from a distinguished statesman, the Honorable Henry Laurens of Charleston. It is generally agreed by local historians that the name was chosen by an early Laurens judge, Jonathan Downs.

Cherokee Indians were the first known inhabitants of the area. Laurens County was originally a part of their hunting territory, and the Cherokees frequently traveled trade routes and well-worn paths leading to fish dams on the rivers.

John Duncan, a native of Aberdeen, Scotland, migrated to Pennsylvania and then found his way to Carolina "back country" c. 1750, settling on Duncan's Creek. Duncan returned to Pennsylvania and enticed friends to join him in his Carolina paradise.

South Carolina Governor James Glen signed a second treaty with the Cherokees in 1755 and thus opened upper Carolina for development. Pioneers continued to migrate from Pennsylvania, Virginia, North Carolina, England, Ireland, and Germany. Some came south to find less crowded or cheap land while others came across the ocean to escape religious or economic oppression. The homesteaders were not disappointed when they discovered dense forests in which game abounded, rich grazing lands, fertile soils, swift rivers, and bold streams.

Often labeled as "crude and downright tough," the upcountry men cleared land, planted crops, constructed sturdy cabins, and faced hardships as well as Indian attacks. Despite the 1755 treaty, the Cherokees waged war in 1759.

Soon after arriving the settlers constructed brush arbors to be used as places of worship. Eventually substantial meeting houses or churches representing various denominations replaced the crude arbors throughout the county. The principal settlements within the limits of Laurens County during the era of the Revolution were located on Duncan's Creek, Reedy River, and Little River.

During the American Revolution, loyalties were divided. Many upcountrymen, especially those who had received large grants from the king, remained loyal to England and thus became known as Tories. On the other hand, Whigs supported the cause of the 13 colonies and their efforts helped to achieve America's independence in 1783.

Significant Revolutionary battles were fought on Laurens soil and stories relating to Laurens names of Cunningham, Musgrove, Langston, Williams, Dillard, Farrow, and Downs, as well as countless others, have been passed down through generations.

With peace, restored manor houses replaced log cabins and villages began to spring up, usually near "meeting houses" and business establishments. Cross Hill, Waterloo, Milton, Princeton, Owings, Ora, Mountville, Gray Court, Clinton, and Laurens became busy trading centers. "Laurensville" was chosen as the county seat and the first recorded court was held in 1785; the first courthouse was constructed of logs. A second courthouse was constructed in 1815 and was replaced in 1840 by the present structure, with additions made in 1857. From 1785 to 1860, the county increased steadily in population and prosperity. The growth of population was due to natural increase and immigration combined.

"Transportation facilities, both public and private were, up until 1850, quite meager. Private traveling facilities consisted almost entirely of saddle horse and gigs [two-wheeled vehicles with tops and seating for two], carriages, and buggies being very rare. Good home raised horses abounded, and young men trained them to 'tote double,' so that they could take girls behind them to church, party or picnic," wrote W.W. Kennedy in an article published in the *Laurens Advertiser* in 1900. "Before the building of railroads in the upcountry passengers and mails were transported in stage coaches, coaches and horses being owned by companies. There were relay stations, usually about ten miles apart, where fresh horses were harnessed awaiting the arrival of the stage so that the change could be made with the minimum of delay. The few merchants went to Charleston in their gigs to buy goods, which were hauled by wagons kept on the road for that purpose."

Prior to the Civil War, the county's public school system was inadequate. There were, however, private schools, academies, and institutions of higher learning.

Laurens was primarily an agricultural county and because cotton was in demand, planters and small farmers continued to expand their acreage with little thought given to industry. The plantation system flourished and slavery expanded along with cotton. By 1860, there were 1,919 slaves in Laurens County along with marked racial problems.

"When the 'craze of secession' swept over the state in 1860, Laurens County took her full share, as she did of the consequences that followed in four years of bloody war, and twenty years of deconstructive reconstruction. She was also ready when the time came for the 'Prostrate State' to rise in 1876 to do her full duty to rid South Carolina of Radical Republicans," wrote Kennedy.

As stated earlier, there was little industry in Laurens County prior to the 1800s. This however changed in 1895 as textile mills were established in Laurens and Clinton. Mills opened their doors and attracted rural citizens seeking employment. Textile villages emerged in Laurens, Clinton, and Joanna.

"In peace their combined wisdom and energy have advanced education and industry, and strengthened our system of self-government, while in war their matchless courage has combined in achievements that have dazzled the world, and their priceless blood has mingled to stain every battlefield on which American arms have contended. The people we have today are the descendants of those Whigs and of those Tories and of their kin who have come across the ocean since the Revolutionary War, and a better people than they do not live under the sun," wrote W.W. Kennedy in 1900. "The Piedmont section of South Carolina is the garden spot of the Southern States, and Laurens County in the midst of this section, is in every respect—people, material resources, and general capabilities—the equal of the best."

One

LAURENS

SITGREAVES HOUSE. Born in 1862, Edwin Broyles Sitgreaves came to Laurens from Tennessee. As a young man he operated the most attractive dry goods store in Laurens and was also involved in real estate. Edwin was married to the former Centellia Martin of Laurens and they were the parents of Mrs. John T. Stevens, Mrs. Edgar Brown, and Osie M. Sitgreaves. Located on Farley Avenue in the city of Laurens, this Victorian home was built by Broyles Sitgreaves, c. 1907. (Courtesy Mrs. Cathryn Sitgreaves Jefferies.)

DINING ROOM. This photograph, taken from the gate of the old jail yard, shows vintage trucks and automobiles and the Dining Room, a Laurens restaurant, in the background. Unidentified gentlemen visit in front of the eating establishment. (Courtesy James H. Gambrell.)

LAURENS BUSINESSMAN. Charles Duckett, an African-American businessman, owned and operated a lumber company and funeral home. The funeral home was located on West Laurens Street and the lumber company on College Place. Duckett is shown here with his truck on West Laurens Street. (Courtesy James H. Gambrell.)

LAURENS EDUCATOR AND WRITER. The daughter of Hattie and Tom Golden, Dr. Mary Whitner was born in Laurens County and lived in a small Victorian cottage on Caroline Street. The Laurens educator taught countless children at the Hampton Street School and was active in St. Paul Baptist Church all of her life. She was also a writer for the *Laurens County Advertiser*, where she reported community happenings and events. (Courtesy Rhodes Collection.)

TRAVELING PHOTOGRAPHER. With camera and goat cart, a traveling photographer visited the Parris home at Laurens Mills in 1946. Looking a little apprehensive but posing nevertheless are, from left to right, (standing) Betty and Mary Parris; (seated in the cart) Sara and Bobby Parris. (Courtesy Mrs. Betty Parris Walker.)

BENEDICT COLLEGE GRADUATE. Born in 1886, Nannie Allison grew up on the the west side of Laurens on the Allison Farm. She inherited the farm from her grandmother Leah, a slave who belonged to the Allison family. "Miss Nannie" was a member of the first graduating class of Benedict College in Columbia. She taught first through tenth grade at Milam Branch, a one-room school, for which she was paid $18 a month. Miss Nannie is remembered as a civic leader, educator, and a link in the chain of African-American history. (Courtesy Rhodes Collection.)

EUELL TAYLOR AND DAUGHTERS. Euell Taylor is pictured here with three of his daughters, Jessie Euell Taylor Tumblin, Arva Taylor McAbee, and Mamie Taylor Bishop. Euell was a descendent of the Taylor family that emigrated from Ireland to settle in the Rocky Springs section of Laurens County. (Courtesy Mrs. Dianne Ginn Clarke.)

NIGHT WATCHMAN. Hal and Estelle Taylor Simmons, the parents of eight children—Shirley Mae, Jack, Jim, Ray, Darrell, Helen, Geneva, and Joann—are shown on the porch of their home in the Riverside area of Laurens. Hal was a night watchman for Laurens Cotton Mills and Estelle was a homemaker. (Courtesy Mrs. Dianne Ginn Clarke.)

PRESBYTERIAN MANSE. The first manse for the Laurens First Presbyterian Church was located on East Hampton Street and was the last house in Laurens to be constructed using slave labor. After the War between the States, a new manse was built closer to the church, and the house on Hampton Street was sold to William Lewers Boyd, who added a second story to the dwelling. Boyd was a descendent of Samuel Lewers, the first pastor of the Laurensville Presbyterian Church. (Courtesy Rhodes Collection.)

PEACE OFFICER. John T. Langston, a Confederate veteran, was a member of the old Third South Carolina Regiment and was known as a soldier of great courage and valor. For many years he served as a peace officer of the city and county of Laurens in various capacities and was a faithful public servant. At the time of his death, he was survived by his children, Mace, Jim, and Bettie Langston, and Mrs. L. Dunk Curry. (Courtesy David Peden.)

LAURENS COUNTY SHERIFF. A veteran of World War I, Caldwell Wardlaw Wier was married to Elizabeth Copeland, and both were both descendants of early families in the Jacks Township. A highly respected law enforcement official, Wier is shown standing in front of the old Laurens County jail. The Laurens Hotel and an early streetlight can also be seen in the background. (Courtesy Robert H. Roper III.)

CRAINE TEXACO. Located on North Harper Street just off the Laurens Public Square, Craine's Texaco Service Station was operated by Bryan Craine. The proprietor offered his customers full service, including oil, water, and tire checks, windshield washing, gas pumping, and simple repairs. (Courtesy Darrell Craine.)

WHAM HOME. Once located on South Harper Street Extension, this Victorian structure was the home of Sallie Coleman and John Wham. The Whams were the grandparents of the late Mrs. Wilma Monroe of Laurens. (Courtesy the late Mrs. Mary Wilma Wham Monroe.)

GEORGIA TECH STUDENTS. Mason Theodore Motes (center) and his classmates stand in front of the dining hall on the Georgia Tech Campus. The son of Nancy Jane and Mace Motes, Mason later married Louise Holmes of Johnston and purchased the historic Governor Simpson home on West Main Street in Laurens. (Courtesy Mason T. Motes.)

NATIVE OF CROSS KEYS. George Washington Garrett was born in the Cross Keys section of Spartanburg and was married to Vida Davis, a native of the same area. Garrett constructed a two-story home on North Harper Street and moved his family there in 1913. (Courtesy Mrs. Ernestine Garrett Starnes.)

NORTH HARPER STREET RESIDENT. Mrs. Vida Davis Garrett and her husband, George Washington Garrett, lived in a two-story, Victorian-style home on North Harper Street. Their children, Mabel Garrett Mims, Lillian Garrett Edwards, and Ernest Garrett, spent their childhood days in the old home. (Courtesy Mrs. Ernestine Garrett Starnes.)

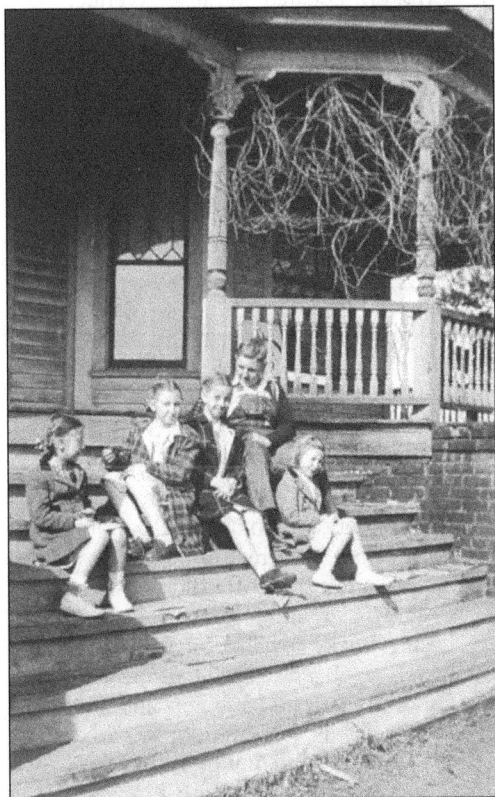

GARRETT GRANDCHILDREN. George and Vida Davis moved into their North Harper Street home in 1913. Their grandchildren, Ernestine, Marjorie, Thelma, Joe, and Elizabeth, are shown sitting on the steps of the family home. (Courtesy Mrs. Ernestine Garrett Starnes.)

GRACE COVENANT PRESBYTERIAN CHURCH. Located on Lucas Avenue, the Church was first organized as the Watts Mill Presbyterian Sunday School in 1924. Before that time, an occasional Presbyterian service was held in the community church building. Eighty-one people were present for the organization of the Sunday School. (Courtesy James L. Cooper Jr. Collection.)

WATTSVILLE CHILDREN AT PLAY. Pictured at 21 Simmons Street in the 1930s are, from left to right, Mildred Fowler, Billie Fowler, and Johnnie Ruth Fowler. Leslie (Buck) Fowler is sitting in the car, which belonged to Fred Earl Brown. The children's parents were Lela and Louis V. Fowler. Louis was a well-know barber in the Wattsville community. (Courtesy Mrs. Johnnie Ruth Fowler Cash.)

COW STALLS. Residents of Watts Mill Village were allowed to keep milk cows, and the mill provided stalls for the animals as well as a pasture. Children often brought the cows in from the pasture to be milked. Mildred and Johnnie Ruth Fowler are shown with their father, Louis, and the family milk cow in front of the Watts Mill cow stalls. (Courtesy Ms. Johnnie Ruth Fowler Cash.)

MOTHER AND DAUGHTER. Carrie Virginia Brown, originally from Darlington County, moved with her family to the Watts Mill community in the late 1800s. Brown is shown here with her daughter Alice Hyler Brown. Carrie later married John Bramlett, who was one of the first church officers of Grace Covenant Presbyterian Church on Lucas Avenue. (Courtesy Rhodes Collection.)

LAURENS COUPLE. Originally from Del Rio, Tennessee, Neil and Ethel Dockery settled in the Watts Mill section of Laurens County in the early 1940s. They were the parents of three children: Paula, Ronnie, and Carolyn. (Courtesy Mrs. Paula Dockery Aiken.)

WATTS HOUSE. Originally a part of the Watts Plantation, this two-story house later became the Watts Mill Community Center. Miss Bettie Richards served as hostess, and the house was used for meetings, parties, classes, and other village functions. Before bathrooms were installed in the village houses, community showers were located in the Lucas Avenue house. (Courtesy James L. Cooper Jr. Collection.)

WATTSVILLE MOTHERS' CLUB. Miss Bettie Richards organized the Wattsville Mothers' Club, which met in the Watts House. Club members of the 1950s are pictured, from left to right, (front row) Inez Cox, Geneva Cox, Oradell Cook, Nellie Davis, Helen Rogers, Irene Owens, and Edith Brewington; (back row) Ruby Curry, Nell Quinn, Lanette Benjamin, Mildred Taylor, Louise Campbell, Dollie Gwinn, Loree Lyons, and Bettie Richards. (Courtesy Mrs. Myrna Benjamin Self.)

GRACIOUS LADY. Skinned knees and elbows, sprained ankles, stubbed toes, and a myriad of other injuries all received kind words from "Miss Bettie." Having been in charge of the community building for many years, she was like a second mother to many children in the Wattsville community. Originally from Liberty Hill, Miss Bettie possessed a sense of humor and was loved by all who knew her. (Courtesy Mrs. Marcel Weeks Lambert.)

21

FORD TEACHER. Miss Mary Senn Efird, a Winthrop graduate, is shown in her classroom at Ford School in the Watts Mill community, where she taught history. Mary later married Daniel Ellis Efird of Lexington County. (Courtesy Nathaniel Bruce Senn III.)

BOYS SITTING ON A WALL. Sitting on the wall in front of the Watts Mill Community Building was a favorite pastime for young men of the textile village. From left to right are Charles Adams, Stanley Leon Johnson, Dean Lyles, Sonny Timmerman, Dan Bowers, Don Bowers, John Henry Owens, Nyles Pulley, Pete Hedgepath, Rowland Craine, Tommy Cox, and unidentified. (Courtesy Mrs. Frances Weathers.)

ALICE BLAKELY WEEKS. Born in 1865, Alice Blakely was the daughter of H. Pickney and Eliott Milam Blakely and the wife of Joseph C. Weeks, who was born in 1858. The couple had five sons, R.F., J.R., Lee, Frank, and Larry, and three daughters, Lila Weeks Burns, Lillie Weeks, and Lula Weeks Collins. (Courtesy Nathaniel Bruce Senn III.)

REMEMBERED WATTSVILLE COUPLE. Larry Weeks and his wife, the former Emma Satterwhite, made their home in the Wattsville community and were the parents of daughters Betty Jo Weeks Curry and Marcel Weeks Lambert. The members of the Weeks family were active members of Grace Covenant Presbyterian Church, where Larry served as elder. He was also active in community organizations, including the Lions Club and Boy Scouts. "Em" and Larry live in the memory of those who knew them. (Courtesy Mrs. Betty Jo Curry Weeks.)

GREGORY FAMILY. Gertrude Brown Gregory was the daughter of Henry and Edney Shirley Brown, originally of Darlington. After arriving in Laurens, Gertrude was married to L.G. Gregory. Gertrude is shown here with her daughters, Ruth, Rosa, and Mamie. The Gregory family lived in the Wattsville community. (Courtesy James Julian Coats Jr.)

A WELL-DRESSED LAD. Young Will Gregory, dressed in the fashion of the day, was the son of Gertrude Brown and L.G. Gregory. (Courtesy James Julian Coats Jr.)

FARMER BROWN. A Furman yearbook reads, "T.C. Brown is a steady fellow from Laurens. He was an outstanding tackle in Fresh football circles last year. He never complains but always fights. He is rightly called 'Farmer' for he can use his hands." The son of Mr. and Mrs. T.B. Brown, T.C. was associated with Brown's Dairy, a family business. The kind and respected gentleman also taught history in the Laurens schools for many years. (Courtesy Dr. Cecil Y. Brown.)

BAILEY SCHOOL. With several grades meeting in just one classroom, teachers in the rural schools taught reading, writing, arithmetic, and spelling to all age levels. The schools were heated with pot-bellied stoves, and trustees usually supplied the school with firewood. The Bailey school was one of many rural schools that dotted the countryside. (Courtesy Laurens County Library.)

CONSTRUCTED BY WILLIAMS. Located on Trinity Church Road, this house was constructed, according to tradition, by Col. John D. Williams, though the exact date of construction is unknown. The two-story home is built of heart pine and has granite steps leading to the front entrance. The sills are 18 inches square and solid pine square posts support the front porch. During the years following the Williams family's occupancy, others, including the Cannon, Knight, Bolt, and Hughes families, have lived in this antebellum house. (Courtesy Rhodes Collection.)

J. HERMAN POWER HOUSE. Booth Knight, a Laurens attorney, constructed this two-story Victorian home, c. 1903, where he lived along with his wife and two children. Handcarved mantles in the parlor and dining room were imported from England. The house was later used as a speakeasy and was known as the "Coconut Grove." J. Herman Power purchased the house and farm in 1939. (Courtesy Laurens County Library.)

CONFEDERATE SOLDIER. A Newberry native, David McKittrick Senn (far right) was a notable citizen of Laurens County and raised a large family of sons and daughters. The Confederate soldier was a member of Company G, Third South Carolina Regiment and was wounded at the Battle of Gettysburg when a mine ball lodged in his elbow. Two Yankee sisters nursed him back to health by applying "cornmeal sacks" to the wound, and then McKittrick walked back to South Carolina. (Courtesy Nathaniel Bruce Senn III.)

W.T. SENN HOME. Located on the Yarborough Mill Road, this two-story house was the home of W.T. and Helen Murphy Senn, the parents of Nathaniel, William, Ben, Harold, Elizabeth Senn Ratchford, Sarah Senn Plowden, and Mary Senn Efird. (Courtesy Nathaniel Bruce Senn III.)

FORMER SERVANT. George Waldrep was once a slave belonging to the family of Elizabeth Arabella Waldrep, who was married to David McKittrick Senn. After the War between the States, George continued to live with the family. Older members of the Senn family recalled the elderly gentleman living in a small house just off Yarborough Mill Road. (Courtesy Nathaniel Bruce Senn III.)

DONATED BRICKS. William T. Senn, the son of Elizabeth Arabella Waldrep and David McKittrick Senn, obtained bricks from an old World War I training camp to construct a farm barn. William, however, donated them to Rocky Springs Presbyterian Church for a new church building. (Courtesy Nathaniel Bruce Senn III.)

FRAME CHURCH BUILDING. Rocky Springs Presbyterian Church was organized in 1780. This frame building, though not the first one to house the church, was constructed in the mid-1800s and served the congregation until a new sanctuary was completed in 1925. (Courtesy Mrs. Betty Waltrip Irwin.)

ROCKY SPRING. In 1780, Rev. John McCosh held a service at a stand in the woods near "the rocky spring" between Clinton and Ora, and this was the beginning of Rocky Springs Presbyterian Church. The first church building was constructed of unhewed logs near the spring, and a second building of logs with a weatherboarded portion was the next church. The third and fourth buildings were constructed in 1820 and 1855, respectively, and both were frame structures. The fifth and present church was erected in 1920. (Courtesy Ken Eargle.)

BELL HOUSE. Robert Bell, a prominent farmer and businessman, taught school for a number of years before becoming a farmer. He was also a director in three banks and was an elder of Rocky Springs Presbyterian Church. Bell left a bequeath of money in his will for the construction of a new church on the condition that the congregation raise a certain amount of money. Bell's wife, the former Rosa Fouche, was instrumental in the erection of the Confederate monument on the Laurens Square. (Courtesy Mrs. Doris Ann Brown Bell.)

COPELAND SCHOOL. This one-room country school was located just off Yarborough Mill Road on the north side of Laurens. The rural school served the educational needs of children in the area. (Courtesy Nathaniel Bruce Senn III.)

COOPER FARMHOUSE. In 1915, James L. Cooper Sr. purchased the white farmhouse located on Fleming Mill Road. The house was constructed c. 1865 and, in the years following, a kitchen, screened porch, and pantry were added. Cooper was married to the former Ursula Clark, and they were the parents of Edith Cooper Wingo and James L. Cooper Jr. The Cooper family operated a dairy farm. (Courtesy James L. Cooper Jr. Collection.)

SUNDAY BEST. Dressed in his Sunday best, Tonch Winfrey takes a break from his duties on the James L. Cooper Sr. farm. Complete with cane and hat, Winfrey is probably headed to church. (Courtesy James L. Cooper Jr. Collection.)

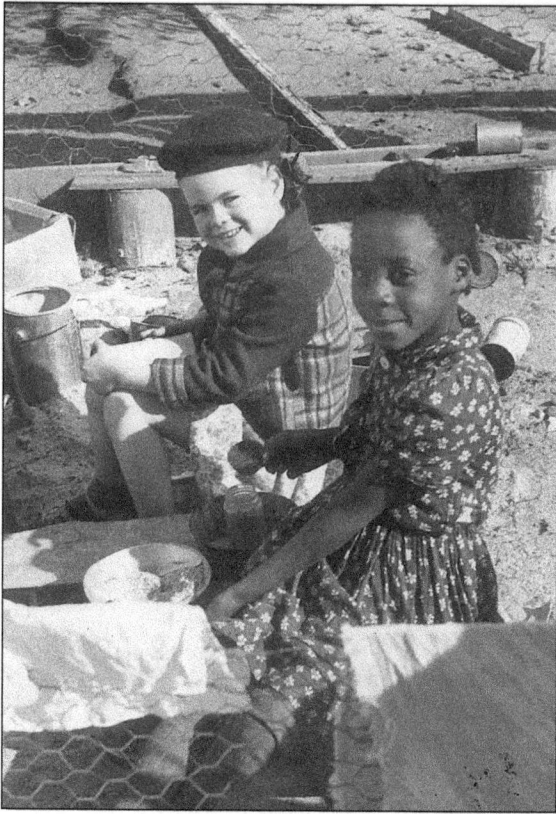

PLAYMATES. Like many other children in rural Laurens County, Emily Wingo Marler and Odessa Harris found entertainment on the family farm. The girls are shown here in the yard of the James L. Cooper Sr. farm. Cooper, Emily's grandfather, was a farmer and dairyman on Fleming Mill Road. (Courtesy James L. Cooper Jr. Collection.)

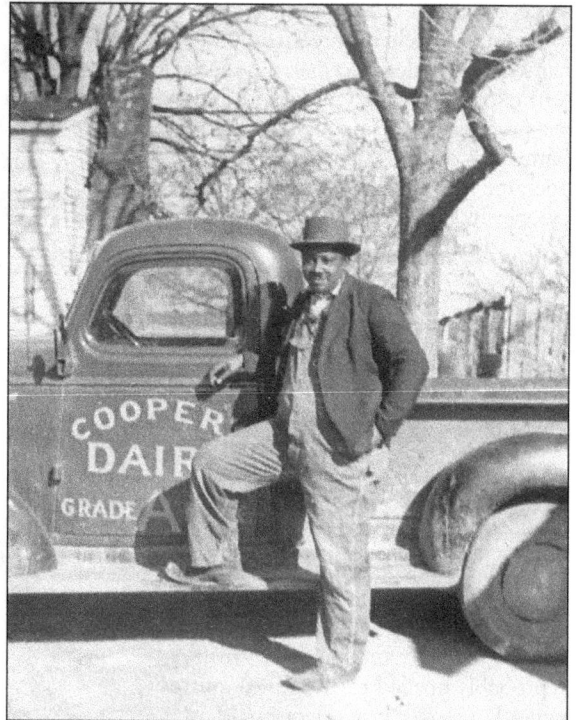

COOPER DAIRY. Ammon Harries, an employee of Cooper Dairy, is shown here with the delivery truck. The pick-up truck replaced the horse-drawn milk wagon and made deliveries faster and easier. (Courtesy James L. Cooper Jr. Collection.)

TILLMAN CREED. Once located on the Princeton Road, the Washington Shell House was a gathering place for politicians. It is said that the upstairs room on the far left was where the Shell Manifesto, or Tillman Creed, was written. Tillman led the Farmer's Movement to victory in the governor's race in 1890, and the creed was his campaign platform. "Wash" Shell was president of the Farmers' Association and an ardent supporter of Gov. Benjamin "Pitchfork Ben" Tillman. (Courtesy Rhodes Collection.)

ALLEN DIAL HOUSE. Allen Dial, grandson of Hastings Dial who settled in Laurens in 1770, constructed this house in 1854 on a site near a stream. After he and his wife died, the house was inherited by nephew Walter Nathaniel Austin. Today the house and farm are owned by Mr. and Mrs. Carrington Herbert. (Courtesy Laurens County Library.)

TRINITY RIDGE SCHOOL. Located in the Trinity Ridge section of Laurens County, this two-story school was a landmark in the community and served many children in the area. (Courtesy Laurens County Library.)

TRINITY RIDGE FARMER. John Warren Tinsley, the son of Zach Hugh and Alice Stone Tinsley, was married to Ruth McDaniel, the daughter of Matthew Lee and Mattie Nichols McDaniel. Upon his father's death in 1926, Warren took over the supervision of the family farm. Warren and Ruth were the parents of three daughters and one son. Standing beside the Zach Tinsley home, built c. 1924, are, from left to right, Ruth, Warren, and an unidentified lady. (Courtesy Mrs. Betty Waltrip Irwin.)

EMMA LANGSTON MOTES. Emma was the daughter of William and Sarah Smith Langston. Her father, born in the vicinity of Langston Baptist Church, settled at Maddens Station, and the family became members of New Prospect Baptist Church. William served as a probate judge for Laurens County. Emma was married to John Motes and they were the parents of five children: Bess Motes Shaw, Mary Motes Sims, John Motes, George Motes, Mace Motes, and Rush Motes. (Courtesy Mason T. Motes.)

JOHN MOTES. Born in 1847, John Motes of the Maddens Station community was married to the former Emma Langston, and they were members of New Prospect Baptist Church. John and his family lived in the Watts House on Lucas Avenue in the Wattsville section of Laurens. John died in 1885. (Courtesy Mason T. Motes.)

PROSPECT SCHOOL. Chalkboards, pictures of United States presidents, and wrought-iron desks with ink wells graced early rural schools, which were heated by pot-bellied stoves. Teachers or chosen students arrived at school early to start the fire in the stove. This 1912 photograph shows the inside of Prospect School. (Courtesy Laurens County Library.)

PEACH FARMER. For many years, Ernest L. Coggins was a noted peach farmer in Laurens County. The orchards and packing shed were operated by Mr. and Mrs. Coggins, their son Brock, and other family members. As well as delicious peaches, the peach orchard provided summer jobs for many Laurens County teenagers. (Courtesy Rhodes Collection.)

Two

Dials

J.N. Leake Residence. This two-story house, located on the east side of Gray Court, was constructed in the 1800s by Dr. Jerome Christopher, who used the house as an office—he was the town's first resident doctor. He often called on his patients in a horse and buggy. Dr. Christopher also served as an alderman. The Leake, Shell, Martin, and Vandaveer families have also called this Victorian house "home." (Courtesy Laurens County Library.)

J. N. LEAK'S RESIDENCE, GRAY COURT, S. C.

AGRICULTURAL TRADING CENTER. The railroad helped to make Gray Court an agricultural trading center. With the depot located on Main Street, Gray Court became a bustling little farming town that was especially lively on weekends. People gathered there to shop, catch the train, and visit with neighbors. Grocery, clothing, general merchandise, and hardware stores lined Main Street, and in the early days, a bank, car dealership, blacksmith shop, and three doctors were also part of the town. (Courtesy Laurens County Library.)

Baptist Church, Gray Court, S.C.

GRAY COURT BAPTIST CHURCH. In August 1912, a small number of Baptists met in the Gray Court Owings School building and, after a sermon by Rev. H.L. Baggott, held an informal conference, during which they resolved to unite in the constitution of a Baptist church. In September 1912, the small group of 39 officially organized the Gray Court Baptist Church, and by November of that same year, the church building had been constructed and the first worship service held. (Courtesy Laurens County Library.)

GRAY COURT UNITED METHODIST CHURCH. Gray Court Methodist Church was organized in 1890 with most of its members coming from Dials United Methodist Church. A large square one-room structure was built in 1891 to house the congregation. The land on which the church was built, comprising approximately two acres, was purchased from R.L. Gray Sr. for $50 per acre. (Courtesy Laurens County Library.)

DIALS METHODIST CHURCH. From left to right and with church bulletins in their pockets, Reverend Singleton, Dunk Curry, Festus Curry, and States Curry pose in front of the historic church that was once called Dials Methodist Society. (Courtesy Mrs. Sarah Jane Limehouse Armstrong.)

CHURCH GROUP. Members of the historic Dials Methodist Church, *c.* 1920, sit on the steps of the old wooden structure. Included in the photograph are Mattie Simmons, John Rhodes Curry, Mavis Claire Curry, Ida E. Curry, Lydie Armstrong, Ethel Armstrong, ? Simmons, Marie Simmons, Grace Owings, Dial Gray, Lola Weathers Campbell, Emma Harris, Inez Willis, Lilly Thomason, Fannette Thomason, Sue Thomason, Jewel Curry Gray, Ilene Curry, Kate Armstrong, and Ora Armstrong. (Courtesy Mrs. Sarah Jane Limehouse Armstrong.)

GRAY COURT PRESBYTERIAN CHURCH. This small wooden church once served the religious needs of Presbyterians in Gray Court. It was one of several churches located in the community. (Courtesy Mrs. Sarah Jane Limehouse Armstrong.)

H.G. ARMSTRONG STORE. Homer G. Armstrong was born in the Dials community of Laurens County and lived in that vicinity his entire life. The son of Dock and Lucinda Robinson Armstrong, Homer was first married to Lula Ball and later to Annie Sue Tollison, both natives of the same community. Homer, a farmer and businessman, is pictured here with Annie in front of his store in Gray Court. (Courtesy Mrs. Linda Armstrong Finley.)

REEVES STORE. Located in Dials Township, Reeves Store was one of many crossroads stores that dotted the landscape of rural Laurens County. Ernest Reeves, a farmer as well as a merchant, was the son of Thaddeus and Emma Gray Reeves and a member of Rabon Creek Baptist Church. Friends and neighbors often gathered in country stores to shop, play a friendly game of checkers, or discuss politics and crops around the stove. (Courtesy Rhodes Collection.)

BARKSDALE-NARNIE SCHOOL. Located in the Barksdale community between the towns of Laurens and Gray Court, this old two-story school stood as a landmark for many years. Countless students remembered their school days in the old structure. (Courtesy Rhodes Collection.)

BARKSDALE SCHOOL. Students at Barksdale School pose for a class photograph. (Courtesy Mrs. Sarah Hurley.)

CLASS OF 1926. The members of the graduating class of 1926 stand on the steps of the Gray Court-Owings School. (Courtesy Mrs. Sarah Jane Limehouse Armstrong.)

DIALS SCHOOL. One of the oldest schools in Laurens County, Dials School was named for Dials Church, which was located nearby. The first school was a small one-room structure built by "Uncle Jack" Harris, whose son Robert was the first teacher. Rural schoolchildren of all ages, probably comprising the entire school, stand in front of a later Dials School. (Courtesy Mrs. Sarah Jane Limehouse Armstrong.)

BEN CAMPBELL'S HOMEPLACE.
Descendants of Taylor Campbell
gather at the Ben Taylor homeplace
on Hellams Road in Gray Court
for their annual Campbell reunion.
The Campbell celebration was a time
for family members to visit, sing,
play musical instruments, enjoy
good food, and pay tribute to their
ancestors. The annual tradition
continues today. (Courtesy Charles
E. Hellams Jr.)

CAMPBELL FAMILY. Thomas B.
Campbell was married to Mary
Elmina "Mamie" Godfrey. A proud
farmer, Campbell was also the
proprietor of a general store and
cotton gin. Members of the Dials
community used the rear of the store
as a school for a short time. From
left to right are (front row) T.B.
Campbell holding Clara, Russell, and
Mamie holding Nancy Jane; (back
row) Leila and Mamie's mother.
(Courtesy Charles E. Hellams Jr.)

PROMINENT SETTLERS. Born in 1798, John Hellams was the son of Squire and Ann Coker Hellams and married Jane Abercrombie in 1836. The Hellams were large landowners in Dials Township and one of the first families to settle in that area. (Courtesy Charles E. Hellams Jr.)

PIERCE MOORE HELLAMS HOUSE. Born in 1858, Pierce Moore Hellams, the son of John and Ann Hellams, inherited his father's collection of law books and served his community as a justice of the peace. History tells us that Hellams conducted court proceedings from his home. He and his wife, Mary Mahala Robertson, kept journals and recorded many of the happenings of their lives. Hellams was also known for his penmanship and for assisting his brother John Russell with the Kyzer-Hellams Map of 1883. (Courtesy Charles E. Hellams Jr.)

HELLAMS FAMILY. Pierce Moore Hellams and his wife, Mary Mahala Robertson, lived with their family on Hellams Road in the Gray Court community. The parents of 11 children, the couple were active members of Dials Methodist Church and are buried in the church cemetery. Members of the Hellams family pictured here are, from left to right, Charles Edward, Pierce, Ralph Augustus, John, Laura H. Simmons, and Mary holding Leon. (Courtesy Charles E. Hellams Jr.)

WELL-KNOWN CITIZEN. Francis Rapley Owings, born in 1840, was a well-known and respected citizen from the Owings area of the county. In fact, Owings Station was named in honor of this gentleman. A Confederate veteran, Owings served in Company A, Sixth South Carolina Calvary. (Courtesy Mrs. Sarah Alice Curry Limehouse.)

FOUNDING FAMILY OF OWINGS STATION. Dressed in clothes typical of the 1800s and brandishing long beards and clay pipes, members of the Owings family gather with friends. From left to right are (front row) John Putman, Issac Owings, and Thomas Owings; (back row) Archball Creswell Owings, Martin Owings, Jonathan "Jot" Owings, "Sallie" Ranson Owings, James Burdette, Nancy Dial Owings, Charlotte Willis Owings, and Rapley Owings, who was founder of the town of Owings. (Courtesy Mrs. Martha Hunter Owings Washington.)

ANNIVERSARY CELEBRATION. Francis Rapley Owings and his wife, Susan Abercrombie Owings, gather with family members in 1912 to celebrate their 52nd wedding anniversary. Mr. and Mrs. Owings are standing on the left of the front porch of the Owings home. (Courtesy Mrs. Sarah Jane Limehouse Armstrong.)

WAITING FOR THE PHOTOGRAPHER. Dressed and waiting, the John Rhodes Curry family awaits their photographer on the lawn of their Gray Court home. From left to right are Sallie Owings Curry, wife of John; John Rhodes Curry; Flaud Curry; States Curry; and Townes Curry. John Rhodes later built a second-story addition on to this one-story home. (Courtesy Mrs. Sarah Alice Curry Limehouse.)

FOUNDER OF CURRY'S LAKE. Flaud Curry, the son of John Rhodes and Sallie Owings Curry, married Sarah Maida Gray, c. 1913. Flaud was the founder of Curry's Lake, a popular recreational facility. The couple were the parents of Sarah Alice Curry Limehouse and Gray Rapley Curry. (Courtesy Mrs. Sarah Jane Limehouse Armstrong.)

EQUESTRIAN. Dressed in a riding habit, Sarah Maida Gray Curry, the wife of Flaud Curry, rides her horse near Curry's Lake in the Gray Court community. (Courtesy Mrs. Sarah Jane Limehouse Armstrong.)

REMEMBERED FACILITY. Curry's Lake was established c. 1920 by Flaud Curry. With the help of his wife, children, and grandchildren, Curry turned the lake and its activities into one of the most popular attractions in upstate South Carolina. Swimming, bowling, dancing, games, animals, and pony rides were just a few of the attractions that thrilled both young and old for almost half a century. (Courtesy Mrs. Sarah Jane Limehouse Armstrong.)

HOW MANY COUSINS WILL A DONKEY HOLD? The grandchildren of John Rhodes and Sallie Owings Curry clown around in the yard of the Curry home. They are, from left to right, Richard, Alton, Ethel, Sara Alice, Gray Rapley, Peden Gene, and Justice Curry. (Courtesy Mrs. Sarah Jane Limehouse Armstrong.)

COTTON FARMER. Zach Gray of the Eden's community proudly shows off a bale of cotton from his farm. Standing with Gray are his wife, Alice Cheek Gray, and grandchildren (from left to right) Sarah Alice Curry Limehouse, Nash Gray, and Gray Rapley Curry. (Courtesy Mrs. Sarah Alice Curry Limehouse.)

FASHION OF THE DAY. Donning the fashion of the day, Mrs. Nettie Curry Blackwell, the wife of Rev. D.J. Blackwell, pulls on her glove as she leaves the family home. (Courtesy Mrs. Sarah Jane Limehouse Armstrong.)

GRANDMOTHER EVELENA. Evelena Walker Stoddard spent her entire life in the Gray Court community. She was a devoted mother and grandmother, teaching her children about duties on the farm, as well as canning and preserving. Evelena was the wife of Joseph Stoddard and the mother of Claude Stoddard Sr. (Courtesy Mrs. Gladys Stoddard Henderson.)

GRAY COURT FARMER. Born in 1888, Claude C. Stoddard Sr. was the son of Joseph and Evelena Walker Stoddard. Claude joined the Bethel Grove Church, where he remained active all his life. In the early days, his family would load up the old wagon, head through the woods, over the "knob," and through the hollow to Bethel Grove every Sunday for services. Claude owned and operated a farm where he produced cotton, corn, wheat, soybeans, and many vegetables. (Courtesy Mrs. Gladys Stoddard Henderson.)

MOTHER AND DAUGHTERS. Claude C. and Flossie Stoddard taught their children the value and importance of education and of being devoted a church member. Claude and Flossie were the proud parents of nine children. Maudie Stoddard Childs and Lydia Stoddard are pictured here with their mother, Flossie. (Courtesy Mrs. Gladys Stoddard Henderson.)

Two

WATERLOO

ROSEMONT. Patrick Cunningham arrived in Laurens County from Virginia and settled on what later became known as the Rosemont Plantation. The house located on the plantation was built *c.* 1790 by Cunningham and was destroyed by fire in 1930. Rosemont was known for its acres of flowers, parks, and avenues. The daughter of Robert Cunningham and the granddaughter of Patrick Cunningham, Ann Pamela Cunningham was responsible for the restoration of Mount Vernon, George Washington's boyhood home. (Courtesy Laurens County Library.)

FOWLER FAMILY. Lucinda Clayton Henderson was born in 1857 in the Mt. Pleasant section of the county, where the Henderson family home, which she inherited, was located. Lucinda was first married to James L. Moore and then, in 1892, married William Wesley Fowler. Taken in 1904, this photograph shows Lucinda and William Wesley Fowler (seated) and their children, standing from left to right, James Wesley Fowler; Lue Belle Fowler Hendrix; and Johnie Casper Moore, Lucinda's son from her first marriage. (Courtesy Mrs. Roberta Fowler Stoddard.)

MT. PLEASANT SCHOOL. This group picture of Mt. Pleasant students was taken in the early 1920s. Even though most of the children are identified, space does not permit listing their names. (Courtesy Mrs. Virginia M. Thompson.)

BANK OF WATERLOO. Located 12 miles south of Laurens, the town of Waterloo received its charter in 1885. The community was largely agricultural, growing cotton, wheat, other grains, and vegetables. Most of the business establishments in town were operated by local people and met the needs of farm families. The Bank of Waterloo was an important part of the town. (Courtesy Rhodes Collection.)

WATERLOO SCHOOL. Most of the schools in rural areas were constructed by the men of the community and were usually framed buildings. Children often walked several miles to attend classes that were taught by one teacher. This photograph of the Waterloo School was taken c. 1910. (Courtesy Laurens County Library.)

"Granny Mary." Mary Ruth Moore (b. 1902), the daughter of "Will" Anderson Moore and Corrie Electra Sanders, married Frank Lee McMahan Sr. at her parents' home on Lee Street in Laurens. The couple had five children: Lou Esther Adams, Frank Lee, William Paul, Mary Marcelle, and Thomas Love. Due to the unconditional love and affection she showed her grandchildren, Mary became known as "Granny Mary." She is pictured here with her children, Lou Esther (standing) and Frank Lee. (Courtesy Mrs. Dora Benjamin McMahan.)

A Sight to See. The old McMahan house was constructed by Lou and John Smith in the 1800s in the Mt. Pleasant community. The house was later purchased by Mary Ruth Moore and Frank Lee McMahan Sr., and finally remodeled by Frank Lee and Dora Bell Benjamin McMahan. The couple's children, Linda Carol Waters and Alice Marie Henson, were watching their Uncle Tommy hauling lime when this photograph was taken. (Courtesy Mrs. Dora Benjamin McMahan.)

PROUD MOTHER. Dora Bell Benjamin was born in 1925 to Eula Irene and John Shell Benjamin of the Beaverdam community. Dora married Frank Lee McMahan, the son of Mary Ruth Moore and Frank Lee McMahan Sr., and the couple lived in what came to be known as the McMahan House. Dora Bell and Frank Lee were the parents of four children: Linda Carol Waters, Alice Marie Henson, Rodger Shell, and Fran Lisa Williams. Dora is pictured here with her daughters, Linda (standing) and Alice. (Courtesy Mrs. Dora Benjamin McMahan.)

BUDDIES. Frank Lee McMahan Jr. of the Mount Pleasant section of the county is pictured with his buddy "Shorty" Rice of Laurens. Frank, the son of Mary Ruth Moore and Frank Lee McMahan Sr., served in World War II, where he received good conduct medals, the Combat Infantryman Badge, and a Purple Heart. Frank Lee married Dora Bell Benjamin of the Beaverdam community. (Courtesy Mrs. Dora Benjamin McMahan.)

UNION BAPTIST CHURCH. The church was organized in 1843 on six acres of land deeded for a meetinghouse by Thomas Coates and John Gary, though services had been held in the vicinity prior to 1822. In that year, the Quaker community in the area moved to Indiana but left behind a strong impression of their spiritual devotion; thus, when the church building was erected, it was often refereed to as the Quaker Church. (Courtesy Mrs. Izora Elledge Boiter.)

BIBLE SCHOOL. These unidentified young people pose with their Bible school teachers at the old frame Union Baptist Church located in the Waterloo Township. The historic Baptist church was organized in 1843 and is often refereed to as the Quaker Church. (Courtesy Mrs. Mary Evelyn Elledge Johnson.)

WORKED FOR COMMUNITY. At the outbreak of the Civil War, Confederate soldier Robert Young Josuah Elledge rushed to the aid of his state and served gallantly in Company A, Sixth Regiment, Butler's Brigade Calvary. After the war, he returned to his farm and worked for the good of his community. He married Loretta Cooper and they had four children: John, J.E., Mrs. J. Wade Culbertson, and Mrs. J.N. Elledge. (Courtesy Mrs. Mary Evelyn Elledge Johnson.)

CONFEDERATE SOLDIER. J. Franklin Elledge served in the Confederate army, Company C, 14th Regiment, McGowan's Brigade, Infantry. He died of disease in McPhearsonville, South Carolina; his body was returned home and laid to rest at the old Elledge Cemetery on Reedy River, near Culbertson's Mill. (Courtesy Mrs. Mary Evelyn Elledge Johnson.)

CULBERTSON HOMEPLACE. Located on the old Cold Point to Ware Shoals Road, this two-story farmhouse was home to several generations of Culbertsons. Andrew and Mattie Sue Wells lived in the house and, later, their son John Henry and his family lived in the old family home. (Courtesy James Wyatt Culbertson.)

HORSE AND RIDER. John Henry Culbertson was born in 1872 and lived on the "Andrew Culbertson Place" all his life. A farmer, Culbertson enjoyed the country life and horseback riding, and he and his wife had seven children: Earl, Ruth, Angie, Lois, Nanny, Wells, and James. They were members of Mt. Olive Baptist Church. (Courtesy James Wyatt Culbertson.)

LIFELONG RESIDENT OF MOUNT OLIVE COMMUNITY. Andrew Culbertson (b. 1826) and his wife, Mary Jones Culbertson (b. 1835), were lifelong residents of the Mt. Olive community near the Reedy River. Culbertson family members gather here for a photograph at the Andrew Culbertson home. (Courtesy James Wyatt Culbertson.)

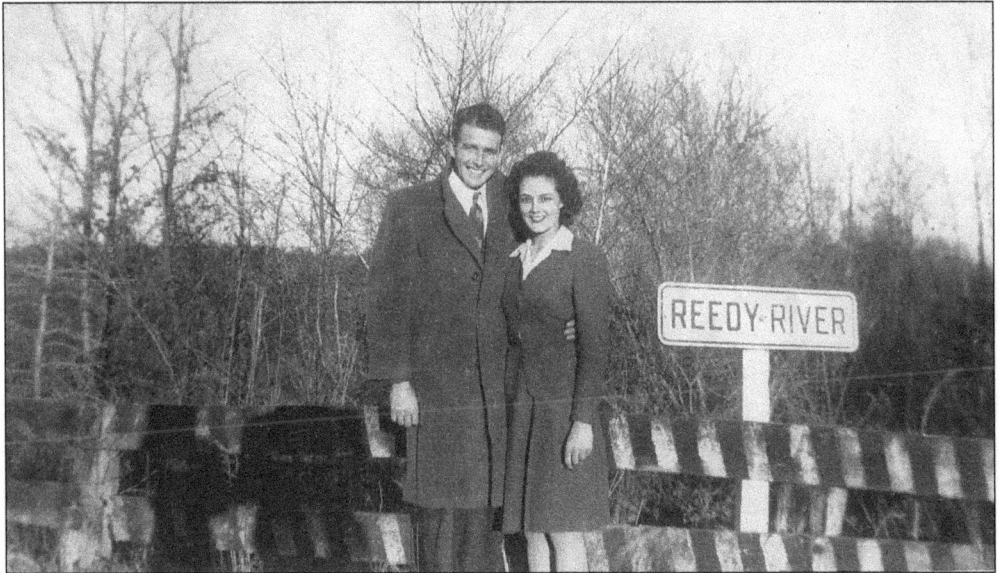

CULBERTSON'S MILL ON REEDY RIVER. Shortly after returning from World War II, James Wyatt Culbertson was photographed with his wife, the former Lois Bradshaw, as the couple stood on the Reedy River Bridge at Culbertson's Mill. From the looks of Culbertson's smile, he is happy to be back on his home soil. The mill is named for Culbertson's ancestors. (Courtesy Mrs. Sue Culbertson Tinney.)

MOUNT OLIVE BAPTIST CHURCH. This church was organized as Pine Ridge Baptist Church in 1891 and held services at the Pine Ridge School. A deed for five acres of land for the church building was conveyed by John W. Knight to Andrew Culbertson, Julian Knight, and F.M. Hughes (trustees), and their successors in office for the sum of $5. In 1892, the name of the church was changed to Mount Olive. (Courtesy James Wyatt Culbertson.)

CENTER POINT SCHOOL. This c. 1934 photograph shows the student enrollment of Center Point School. From left to right are as follows: (front row) Walter Blackwell, ? Stevenson, Clee Blackwell, William Dove, Velma Cooper, Gloria Burton, Charles Ray Chapman, Edward Baldwin, Joe Coker, and Gerald Cooper; (middle row) unidentified, ? Jackson, unidentified, Paul Elmore, and Barron Culbertson; (back row) Miss Emily Taylor, J.B. Freeman, ? Stevens, Brent Culbertson, Mickey Freeman, Edsel Culbertson, Adelle Owens, unidentified, and Lamar Cooper. (Courtesy James Wyatt Culbertson.)

Three

SULLIVAN

TUMBLING SHOALS. This house was constructed in 1820 by Joseph Sullivan (whose father had moved to the area from Virginia) for his bride, Temperance Arnold. Part of the house included a log structure that dated back to 1773 and marks the old homestead as an early outpost in Laurens County. (Courtesy Rhodes Collection.)

BORN IN 1848. Mary Judson Cooper was the wife of John Porter Elledge. Both were descendants of two early Laurens County families well known in the Waterloo and Sullivan Townships. John, a Confederate soldier, was a private in Company C, Third Battalion, Kershaw's Brigade, Infantry and was wounded at Cedar Creek, Virginia. (Courtesy Mrs. Izora Elledge Boiter.)

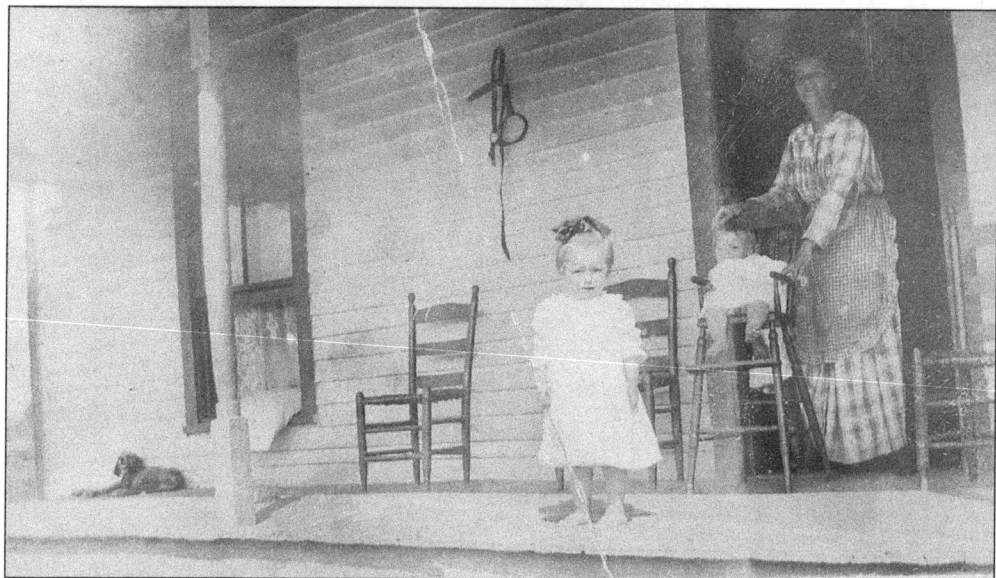

COUNTRY WIFE AND MOTHER. Clad in an apron, Mrs. Emma Elledge, the wife of James Newton Elledge, cares for her daughters, Izora and Julia, on the porch of the family's country home, c. 1918. (Courtesy Mrs. Izora Elledge Boiter.)

FATHER AND DAUGHTER. Emma, whose hair had never been cut, and her father, Robert Elledge are shown in the L.A. McCord Studio in Laurens. Emma later married a cousin, James Newton Elledge. (Courtesy Mrs. Mary Evelyn Elledge Johnson.)

FAMILY GATHERING. F.A. Boiter sits outside his log cabin in the Harmony Church community and is joined by Jerry and Judy Bryant. Dressed in their Sunday best, the trio enjoy a Sunday afternoon in the country. (Courtesy Izora Elledge Boiter.)

65

BLYGH JOHNSON. Originally from the Princeton community and a veteran of World War I, Blygh Crosby Johnson married Mary Evelyn Elledge, the daughter of Emma and James Newton Elledge. The Johnson family made their home in the Hickory Tavern community. (Courtesy Mrs. Mary Evelyn Elledge Johnson.)

SUNDAY DRIVE. Dressed for the occasion, Ernest Boiter of the Hickory Tavern community looks as if he has enjoyed a Sunday afternoon drive through the countryside. Smiling, he poses in front of his Austin automobile, c. 1935. (Courtesy Mrs. Izora Elledge Boiter.)

DAY'S END. Frances Elledge Johnson, Izora Elledge Boiter, and Julia Elledge Bullock, all sisters, hitch a ride at the end of the day's work, c. 1942, on the J.A. Boiter farm in the Hickory Tavern community. (Courtesy Mrs. Izora Elledge Boiter.)

FRIENDSHIP CHURCH. A frame church constructed in 1820 originally served Baptists, Methodists, and Presbyterians in the area. After the Baptist and Methodist congregations moved out, the Presbyterians remained, built another frame church in 1859, and built a brick one in 1953. Dr. W.P. Jacobs, while serving as pastor in 1872, expressed a desire to organize an orphanage. A Friendship lad donated 50 cents to the cause, and Thornwell was the outgrowth of that first contribution. (Courtesy Rhodes Collection.)

TUMBLING SHOALS POWER PLANT. Located on the Reedy River in the Sullivan Township of Laurens County, the Tumbling Shoals Power Plant provided citizens with electric current adequate for their increasing needs. (Courtesy Mrs. Izora Elledge Boiter.)

SUPERINTENDENT. James Elledge, the superintendent of the Tumbling Shoals Power Plant, stands in the door of the powerhouse around 1935. (Courtesy Mrs. Izora Elledge Boiter.)

SUPERINTENDENT'S HOUSE. Izora Elledge Boiter, the daughter of James Elledge, feeds the family hog in the yard of the Tumbling Shoal's superintendent's house. The chickens, cat, and backyard well add to the country charm of the house. Izora's father was superintendent of the plant. (Courtesy Izora Elledge Boiter.)

BOYD'S MILL ON REEDY RIVER. On his way to Ware Shoals, Nathaniel Dial spotted a falls at Boyd's Mill on Reedy River. He made plans to develop this natural resource in order to replace the Laurens steam plant, which was inadequate. With the help of two other townsmen, Dial formed the Reedy River Power Company. (Courtesy Mrs. Izora Elledge Boiter.)

REEDY RIVER BRIDGE. The old Reedy River Bridge was located on Highway 76 in Sullivan Township. It, like most of the other steel bridges in Laurens County, is now a thing of the past. (Courtesy Rhodes Collection.)

HICKORY TAVERN SCHOOL. Probably taken in the 1950s, this yearbook picture shows a group of Hickory Tavern High School students posing in front of their school. (Courtesy Mrs. Mary Evelyn Elledge Johnson.)

Dear Old Golden Rule Days. Captured *c.* 1935, this unidentified group of students and teachers are shown in front of the brick columns of the old Hickory Tavern School. (Courtesy Mrs. Izora Elledge Boiter.)

Eighth-grade Class. Eighth-grade students sit on the bleachers in the gymnasium of the Hickory Tavern School for a class photograph. They are shown with their teacher Justice Curry. (Courtesy Rev. Gene Curry.)

SCHOOL FRIENDS. Hickory Tavern High School students stand for a class picture in front of the old Hickory Tavern School. The photographer probably snapped these classmates in the 1930s. (Courtesy Mrs. Izora Elledge Boiter.)

JOHN BALENTINE HOUSE. John Balentine acquired this two-story house and a vast amount of acreage in 1843 from John Milam who, with his wife, Molly, had moved to Mississippi. From the second-floor windows, Balentine could view the operations of his plantation. Born in 1800, Balentine had 17 children and, at the time of his death in 1884, 54 grandchildren, among them Dr. D.W. Daniel of Clemson College and William Balentine, the founder of Balentine Packing Company in Greenville. (Courtesy Laurens County Library.)

Four

SCUFFLETOWN

MUSGROVE HOUSE. The plantation manor house of the Musgrove family was constructed on a hill overlooking the Enoree River prior to the mid-1770s. The home was a two-story frame construction with a porch extending across the front of the first floor and down one side. Chimneys marked each end. Maj. Edward Musgrove, the builder, remained loyal to England during the Revolutionary War, but his children were divided in their sympathies. Musgrove's daughter Mary distinguished herself as a Revolutionary War heroine by aiding the Whigs. (Courtesy Rhodes Collection.)

MUSGROVE MILLS. This early postcard shows a bird's-eye view of the Musgrove vicinity, including the mills, dam, and bridge. Named for an early settler, the Musgrove area was the site of the Revolutionary War battle of Musgrove Mills. (Courtesy Laurens County Library.)

ORA ASSOCIATED REFORMED PRESBYTERIAN (ARP) CHURCH. This congregation was organized around 1790 and was originally listed as Madole's Old Field Church. Services were held in a small log house approximately 500 feet from the church's present location. By 1809, the name was changed to Warrior Creek because of a nearby stream, and in 1836, it was changed again, this time to Bethel. The church eventually became know as Ora Associated Reformed Presbyterian Church. (Courtesy Laurens County Library.)

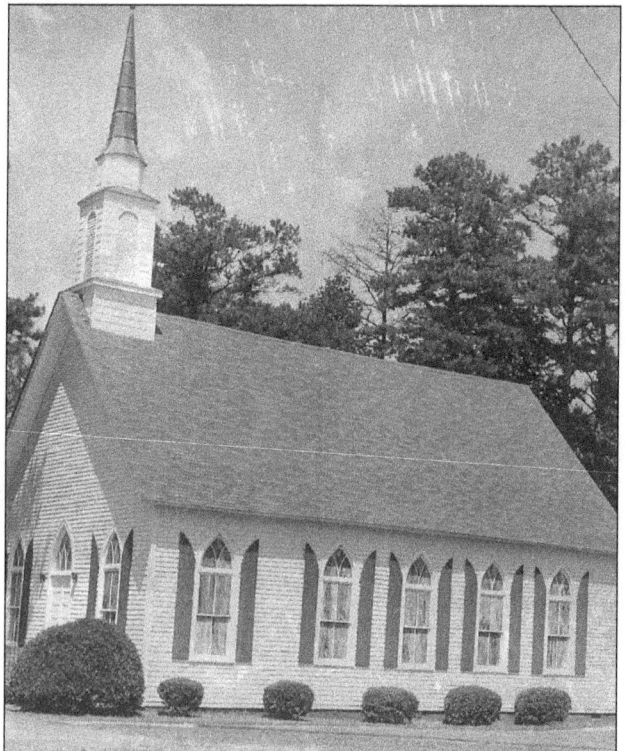

AN ORA CHILD. T. Craig Hunter was born in Ora in 1895 to Leander and Mattie Craig Hunter. Married to Leonard Owings of the Owings community, T. Craig Hunter is buried in the Ora ARP Church cemetery. (Courtesy Mrs. Martha Hunter Owings Washington)

PATTERSON CHAPEL. Organized in 1866, this congregation held their first services in a brush arbor. Later services were held in the Grapevine Schoolhouse, which was made of logs and furnished with slab benches and a crude desk. The first church building was erected in 1886 and named for the Patterson family. (Courtesy Laurens County Library.)

SETTLED ON MARTIN POOLE PLACE. Mrs. Jennie Rose Hunter Reeder was born in the Ora section of the county in 1898 and was married to Spurgeon Reeder Sr. on Christmas day in 1919. The couple settled on the "Martin Poole Place" in the Sandy Springs community and parented four children: Maude Reeder Barnes, Mary Reeder Hill, Spurgeon Reeder Jr., and Josephine Reeder Sullivan. (Courtesy Rhodes Collection.)

SPURGEON REEDER SR. Born in the Oak Grove section of Laurens County in 1898, Spurgeon Reeder was married to the former Jennie Rose Hunter after meeting her at a church service. Spurgeon was an active member of Duncan Creek Baptist Church. In 1949, the Reeder family moved to the Nannie Allison farm, west of Laurens. (Courtesy Rhodes Collection.)

CLARK FAMILY. Members of the Clark family are pictured outside their home, which was located in the vicinity of Langston Baptist Church. Seated are Tirzah Langston Clark and her husband, John Clark. Tirzah was the sixth child of John and Mary Mason Langston and was born in 1839. John Clark's family came from Rhode Island and had been pioneer manufacturers in Spartanburg County. Standing behind the couple, from left to right, are their children, Janie Caroline Clark Holland, William Barnett Clark, Mary Emma Clark Cooper, and John Mason Clark. (Courtesy David Holland.)

THE CLARK FAMILY HOME. Located above the North Fork of Duncan Creek and constructed in the late 1700s, this home was owned by the family of John W. Clark and his descendants for several generations. John Clark is credited with establishing the first small cotton mill in upstate South Carolina. Janie Clark, a descendant, married Reese L. Holland, and with the passing of years, the structure became known as the Holland House. It was one of the last self-sufficient farms in Laurens County. (Courtesy Rhodes Collection.)

WELL HOUSE. One of many buildings necessary for the survival of a plantation, the well of this three-story Reese L. Holland home stood in the yard. Other outside buildings included a carriage house, a large barn, a servants' house, a chicken house, and a blacksmith shop. The buildings were constructed of hand-planed boards and put together with hand-forged nails. A path embedded with smooth stones taken from Duncan's Creek led from the dwelling to the carriage house. (Courtesy Rhodes Collection.)

CABIN ON REESE HOLLAND FARM. This two-room house, used by servants, was constructed of poplar and oak logs, shaped with a broad ax and an adz, and the roof was made of split shingles. A worn granite step stood at the front entrance of the cabin. (Courtesy Rhodes Collection.)

HOLLAND FAMILY. Janie Clark and Reese Holland visited a photography studio with their children, John Bluford and T. Craig, to sit for a family portrait. Reese Holland was a well-known farmer near Langston Baptist Church. (Courtesy David Holland.)

LAURENS COUNTY FARMER. Reese Holland, the son of Margaret Adair Holland and Bluford Holland, married Janie Clark, and the couple lived in Janie's ancestral home, which became known as the Holland House. They were the parents of two children, T. Craig and John Bluford. Reese Holland operated one of the last self-sufficient farms located in the Langston community of Laurens County. (Courtesy James L. Cooper Jr. Collection.)

ERSKINE BENJAMIN. A World War I veteran, Erskine Quincy "Bud" Benjamin was born in the early 1900s to Alah Adair and William Reeder Benjamin. Born and raised in Laurens County, Bud was a descendent of the Adair family, one of the first families to settle in Laurens County. (Courtesy Corrie Jackson Grether.)

LANGSTON BAPTIST CHURCH. This church was organized c. 1773. The land was given for the church building by Solomon Langston, a gentleman who lived at the foot of the hill below the church. Solomon was the father of Revolutionary heroine Dicey Langston. Before 1790, the congregation had 141 members. The present church was erected c. 1840. The Langston family cemetery is located near the quaint little church. (Courtesy James L. Cooper Jr. Collection.)

SUBSTANTIAL CITIZEN. John Langston, the fifth son of Henry and Sara Murphy Langston and the grandson of Solomon Langston, was born in 1800. He was first married to Mary Mason, the daughter of David Mason, and then later married Sophia Smith. Langston was a substantial citizen in his community, a member of Langston Baptist Church, and an ardent Baptist. Four sons of John Langston served in the Confederate Army. (Courtesy David Holland.)

CAPTAIN LANGSTON. Capt. David Henry Mason Langston (b. 1834) moved to Clinton in 1854 and engaged in the mercantile business with George P. Copeland. In 1860, Langston assisted in organizing Company I, Third South Carolina Volunteers and was elected first lieutenant and, later, captain. At the battle of Savage's Station in 1862, Langston was wounded three times and little hope was left for his recovery. With his wounds scarcely healed, he was killed at Gettysburg in July 1863 while in command of his regiment. (Courtesy David Holland.)

WOODEN BRIDGE. The Shelton's Mill Bridge crossed Duncan Creek near the old Clark-Holland residence. A gristmill and tan yard were located near the wooden structure. The bridge received its name from the Shelton family that moved to South Carolina from Rhode Island and operated an early cotton mill. (Courtesy David Holland.)

CONFEDERATE VETERANS REUNION. Members of Company F, 14th Regiment, South Carolina Volunteers met at Langston Baptist Church on August 19, 1907 for a reunion. From left to right are as follows: (front row) John Gore, Bill Copeland, Pink Blakely, Bill Donnan, Wren Anderson, Oliver Templeton, Wilson Blakely, unidentified, Jim Sloan, Bill McClary, unidentified, and Jim Dillard; (back row) Will Wright, Will Clark, Dan Yarborough, Bluford Henry, George Hannah, Dr. Will Shands, Joe Todd, Warren Blakely, ? Snead, and three unidentified men. (Courtesy David Holland.)

PLANTED BY THE SIGNS. John and Alexene Davis were tenants on the Dillard farm located on Duncan's Creek. Alexene, who was born on the farm and lived in the area for her entire life, was taught at an early age by her father to read signs from the almanac. She and her husband planted crops, pulled teeth, and predicted the weather by studying the 12 signs of the zodiac and their association with parts of the body. (Courtesy Rhodes Collection.)

AFRICAN-AMERICAN SCHOOL. Following the War between the States, African-American schools began to appear throughout Laurens County. The Long Branch School, constructed in 1908, was one such institution. One teacher generally served the educational needs of children of all ages. (Courtesy Laurens County Library.)

THE PENLANDS. Andrew Penland was born in Slabtown, Tennessee in 1873. He settled in the Oak Grove community of Laurens, married Theopa Mobley of Union (b. 1899), purchased what was known as the Old Sumeral Place, and became a farmer. Andrew and Theopa were the parents of eight sons and one daughter. Andrew is pictured here with his horse at the family home. (Courtesy Mrs. Josie Penland Rhodes.)

COUNTRY LAD. Young Andy Penland, the son of Andrew and Theopa Penland, is shown here with the family milk cow. Along with brothers and a sister, Andy lived on the family farm in the Oak Grove community of Laurens County. A corncrib and small barn appear in the background. (Courtesy Mrs. Josie Penland Rhodes.)

EARLY SETTLERS. Adeline Pitts Duvall was born in 1822 and her husband, John Washington Duvall, was born in 1816. The Duvalls were one of many pioneer families that settled in Laurens County. (Courtesy Mrs. Doris Ann Brown Bell.)

GRANDDAUGHTER. Born in 1970, Ada Eugenia Bell Wingo posed with her grandmother Adeline Pitts Duvall. Ada's mother was Margaret Duvall Bell, and Ada was a member of Rocky Springs Presbyterian Church. (Courtesy Mrs. Doris Ann Brown Bell.)

TYPICAL LAURENS COUNTY HOME.
The style of this two-story frame house
was typical of farmhouses throughout
Laurens County. This one, located
in the Oak Grove community, was
the old home of Jerimiah Leake and
Margaret Duvall Bell. (Courtesy
Mrs. Doris Ann Brown Bell.)

OAK GROVE COMMUNITY COUPLE. William
Holmes Bell (b. 1889) married Aileene Ledford
(b. 1901), the daughter of J.E. and Adda Blakely
Ledford. William served as a private in the
field artillery during World War I. William and
Aileene were the parents of four sons: Robert,
Joseph, William, and James. The Bells were
members of Rocky Springs Presbyterian Church.
(Courtesy Mrs. Doris Ann Brown Bell)

SMITH HIPP PLACE. It is believed that Smith Hipp constructed this two-story farmhouse near Duncan's Creek in the late 1800s. A blacksmith's shop, cotton house, and barn were originally part of the estate. Anderson Senn and his wife, Amelia Hazel Senn, lived in the house after the Hipp family, as did various tenant families. James Julian Coats Sr. and his wife, Alice Brown Coats, purchased the house and surrounding farm in 1933. (Courtesy James Julian Coats Jr.)

OAK GROVE COMMUNITY. Well-known residents of the Oak Grove community pose with friends and family. They are, from left to right, as follows: (front row) Ella Bell, Mr. ? Tillison of Greer, Mabel Goodwin, Ora Bell, Edith Cooper Wingo, Mrs. O.P. Goodwin, Earl Goodwin's wife, and Sen. O.P. Goodwin; (back row) Bryan Goodwin Sr., Irene Goodwin, Mrs. ? Tillison, Mary Goodwin, and Earl Goodwin. (Courtesy Mrs. Doris Ann Brown Bell.)

BELLVIEW BAPTIST CHURCH. Located in the Oak Grove community, Bellview was organized in 1900. Lafayette Ramage, who was reared by his Aunt Sally Bell, gave the congregation 1.625 acres so that a church could be constructed. The land was given with the understanding that the church would be built in view of the Bell home, thus the church was called Bellview. (Courtesy Bellview Baptist Church.)

BELL-RAMAGE-IRWIN HOUSE. When Will and Jessie Irwin purchased this house in 1927, the home had two stories and seven rooms. The original three rooms and loft were likely built by James Bell *c.* 1850. The front two-story section, with four rooms and two halls, was added *c.* 1890 by Lafayette Ramage. The Irwins remodeled the house, which was located four miles northeast of the Laurens Courthouse. (Courtesy Mrs. Betty Waltrip Irwin.)

IRWIN'S DAIRY. When Will Irwin and Jessie Irwin were courting in 1916, little did they dream that they would start a flourishing dairy after they were married. Will was the son of James Samuel and Fannie Morrison Irwin originally of Abbeville County. Jessie was the oldest daughter of Zach Hugh and Nannie Alice Stone Tinsley of Laurens County. The couple was married at Jessie's father's home in the Trinity Ridge community in 1917, and later moved to a farm in the Oak Grove community and organized Irwin's Dairy. (Courtesy Mrs. Betty Waltrip Irwin.)

MILKING BARN. W.F. and Jessie Tinsley Irwin purchased the old Bell-Ramage property in the Oak Grove section in 1927. After remodeling the old home, W.F. built a milk house, calf barn, and other outside buildings. The milking barn was constructed c. 1935. Customers of the couple's Irwin's Dairy declared that "Miss Jessie's chocolate milk was the best ever produced." (Courtesy Mrs. Betty Waltrip Irwin.)

COSTUMED PORTRAIT. Fred Irwin posed for a photographer in a Native American costume that was a gift from his Aunt Margaret and Uncle Means Knight of Laurens. Fred attended the Oak Grove School, Laurens High School, and Clemson University. Irwin served in World War II and was discharged as a captain in 1946 at which time he returned to the family dairy business. (Courtesy Mrs. Betty Waltrip Irwin.)

CONFEDERATE SERVICE MEDAL WINNER. Joseph T. Todd served in Company F, 14th South Carolina Volunteers. Following the war, he married Sarah Ann Reed of Cross Hill and settled on his father's farm in the Long Branch section of the county. Todd first constructed a log cabin and later a house, *c.* 1875, on the site of the cabin, which was moved one-quarter mile to the north and reconstructed. Joseph and Sarah were the parents of eight children. (Courtesy George Lewis Compton Jr.)

Long Branch Couple. George Washington Cunningham (b. 1873) was married to Margaret Elizabeth "Bessie" Todd (b. 1875), the daughter of Joseph T. and Sarah Ann Reed Todd. The couple lived in the old Todd home in the Long Branch section, and with the passing of years, it became known as the Cunningham House. The Cunninghams were the parents of McLeese, Lewis, Corrie Cunningham Compton, and Ethel Cunningham Rowland. (Courtesy George Lewis Compton Jr.)

Four Little Cunninghams. These girls and boys, the children of George W. and Bessie Todd Cunningham, are grouped around a wicker chair for a picture. Born in the early 1900s, the four Cunninghams grew up at the Cunningham farm located in the Long Branch community. From left to right, they are McLeese, Ethel Cunningham Rowland, Corrie Cunningham Compton, and George Lewis. (Courtesy George Lewis Compton Jr.)

MR. AND MRS. SAM COMPTON SR. After their marriage, Samuel Eugene Compton and his wife, the former Corrie Cunningham, resided in the Long Branch community. Sam was a well-known farmer and Corrie a homemaker. They were active members of Rocky Springs Presbyterian Church, where Sam was an elder and Corrie a longtime teacher of the kindergarten class. Four sons, Samuel Eugene Jr., George Lewis, James Todd, and Carol Duvall Compton, were born to the couple. (Courtesy George Lewis Compton Jr.)

CUNNINGHAM KITCHEN, 1940. Alice Todd Simpson Cunningham churns while Minnie Prince Cunningham prepares a meal on the wood stove in the kitchen of the Todd-Cunningham house, located in the Long Branch community. Alice was the second wife of George Cunningham and Minnie the wife of McLeese Cunningham. The Cunningham house and farm originally belonged to the Cunningham grandfather, Joseph Todd. (Courtesy George Lewis Compton Jr.)

Five

HUNTER

VICTORIAN MANSION. The large Victorian mansion located on West Main Street in Clinton was once the home of Sallie Jane Coleman and John Wham. The Wham family later moved to Laurens. Taken in the late 1800s by W.E. Stones' Photographic Studio of Clinton, this photograph shows the Wham family, from left to right, John, Isabell, Fred, and Sallie Jane, standing with their animals on the front lawn. (Courtesy the late Mrs. Mary Wilma Wham Monroe.)

SECOND LARGEST TOWN AND COUNTY. In 1809, Clinton emerged around Holland's Store, which was the only store and post office in the lower part of Laurens County. Five Points, located approximately one mile west of the store, was a gathering place for men because of the horsetrack, bars, and chicken fights. (Courtesy Laurens County Library.)

THE TOWN OF CLINTON. Clinton was chartered in 1864, and in the years following the War between the States, many businesses were established in the town. The town also became the home of Presbyterian College, the Thornwell Home for Children, and the Whitten Center. (Courtesy of Laurens County Library.)

UNION STATION. The railroad arrived in Clinton in 1850 and was a turning point in the survival of this little community, which was later chartered in 1864. Henry Clinton Young, a Laurens attorney, was chairman of the committee appointed to map the streets and rename the little town; thus, it was eventually named in his honor. (Courtesy Miss Elaine Martin.)

CLINTON HOTEL. As in many other small communities, the Clinton Hotel became a landmark. Farmers arriving from rural points in the county, as well as businessmen and traveling salesmen, were frequent guests in the establishment, which was conveniently located near the depot. (Courtesy of Laurens County Library.)

BROAD STREET METHODIST CHURCH. Methodism came to Clinton in 1854 and was one of the first churches of any denomination to be established in the city. This brick church was constructed in 1914 on the corner of North Broad and Ferguson Streets to better serve the needs of the congregation. (Courtesy Miss Elaine Martin.)

FIRST BAPTIST CHURCH OF CLINTON. Plans for building a Baptist church in Clinton were discussed in 1881 by elders M.E. Broadus and R.S. Griffin and others, who met in the Presbyterian church. Three days later the group met again and decided to form a church. There were 20 charter members, and the first worship service was held in 1881 in the Methodist church. Several structures have since served the congregation; the first was a wooden building. (Courtesy Laurens County Library.)

CLINTON'S FIRST PRESBYTERIAN CHURCH. In 1853, Rev. Zelotes Holmes, a minister serving Duncan's Creek Church, believed that the small village of Clinton was large enough to have its own church. A committee was formed in 1855 to organize a church. In 1864, William Jacobs was called as minister. Three buildings have served the Presbyterian congregation, a white wooden-frame church, a stone church constructed in 1904, and the present stone structure that was constructed in 1930. (Courtesy Laurens County Library.)

HOME OF PEACE. While serving as pastor of Clinton's First Presbyterian Church, William Plumer Jacobs built a home for destitute children and named it Thornwell for theologian James Henry Thornwell. In 1875, ten orphaned Confederate children moved into the stone building that came to be know as the House of Peace, and the Thornwell Home for Children was born. Dr. Jacobs served Thornwell until his death in 1917. (Courtesy Laurens County Library.)

General View of Presbyterian College Campus, Clinton, S. C.

PRESBYTERIAN COLLEGE. After becoming pastor of Clinton's First Presbyterian Church and founding the orphanage called Thornwell, Rev. William P. Jacobs turned his attention to education, and Clinton College was established in 1880 primarily for Thornwell children. Through struggles and hardships in the early years, the college survived, remained in Clinton, and, in 1890, became known as Presbyterian College. William S. Lee was the first president of the college. (Courtesy Laurens County Library.)

A GIRL'S JOURNAL. Lizzie Owens, a student at Clinton Female Academy, kept a journal prior to the War between the States in which she recorded town events as well as entries concerning her friends, school, and church. Lizzie married Dr. Thomas Craig of Clinton. (Courtesy Mrs. Martha Hunter Owings Washington.)

FLORIDA STREET SCHOOL. This 1933 photograph shows a group of Florida Street School students. (Courtesy Mrs. Nellie Price Hanvey.)

CLINTON HIGH SCHOOL. The first Clinton High School opened in 1873 with 42 students and became Clinton College in 1880. From the turn of the century until 1917, the school was located on the corner of Elizabeth and Academy Streets. A new high school building, shown above, was erected on Hampton Avenue in 1917. The high school moved into a new facility on North Adair Street in 1956. (Courtesy Laurens County Library.)

HAYS HOSPITAL. This *c.* 1940 postcard shows the Hays Hospital, which was constructed by bricking in and adding on to the J.W. Copeland home on Woodrow and Hampton Streets. The brick structure served the medical needs of Clinton residents and was named in honor of prominent Clinton physician, Dr. S.C. Hays. (Courtesy Miss Elaine Martin.)

VICTORIAN COTTAGE. Henry Vance constructed this Victorian cottage on Centennial Street in Clinton *c.* 1890. The white house has eight gables; the porch and gables are adorned with gingerbread trim. The interior features wainscoting, wide ceiling moldings, and paneled doors. Mrs. John Bluford Holland purchased the house from W.S. Shands in 1956. (Courtesy David Holland.)

LYDIA COTTON MILLS. Lydia Cotton Mills was founded in 1902 in the town of Clinton, and Mercer Silas Bailey served as its president until his death in 1926. Cassius Mercer Bailey became the next president and served until his death in 1935, at which time William James "W.J." Bailey became president. W.J. headed both Lydia and Clinton Mills until his death in 1948. He was succeeded by Putsy S. Bailey, Robert Vance, and later, George Cornelson. (Courtesy Laurens County Library.)

TEXTILE EMPLOYEES. Lydia Cotton Mills was founded in Clinton by the Bailey family in 1902. They had 40 employees operating 4,000 spindles and 150 looms. Shown here are early Lydia employees. (Courtesy Rhodes Collection.)

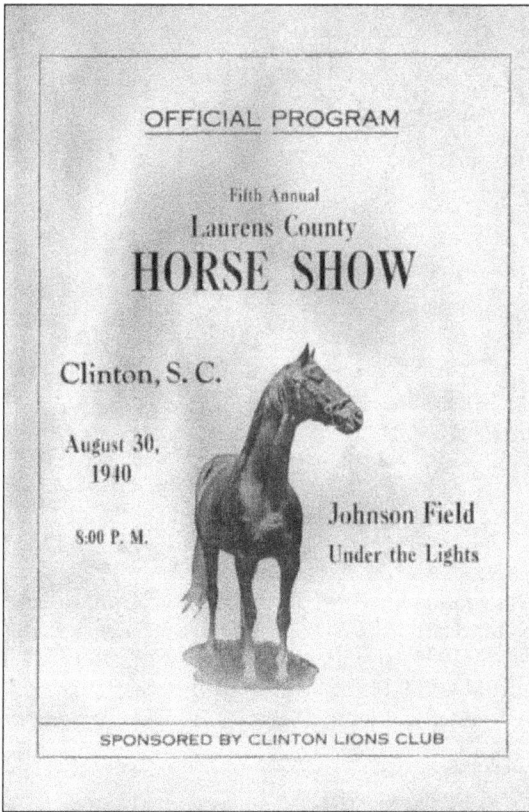

OFFICIAL PROGRAM

Fifth Annual
Laurens County
HORSE SHOW

Clinton, S. C.

August 30,
1940

8:00 P. M.

Johnson Field
Under the Lights

SPONSORED BY CLINTON LIONS CLUB

UNDER THE LIGHTS. The fifth annual Laurens County Horse Show was held in Clinton in 1940 on Johnson Field "under the lights." The show committee was made up of "Peck" Cornwall (chairman), James Addison, Hubert Boyd, Heath Copeland, Edward Henry, Ryan Lawson, Jack Davis Jr., Brooks Owens, P.S. Bailey, and Clyde Lankford. (Courtesy Mrs. Lillian Dillard Stephens.)

KENTUCKY BELLE. Ten-year-old Lillian Dillard joined other equestrians, both young and old, for a Clinton horse show, c. 1939. She and her mare, Kentucky Belle, competed in the Pony Class, 14.2 hands or under. The blue-ribbon winner of the competition received a cup. (Courtesy Mrs. Lillian Dillard Stephens.)

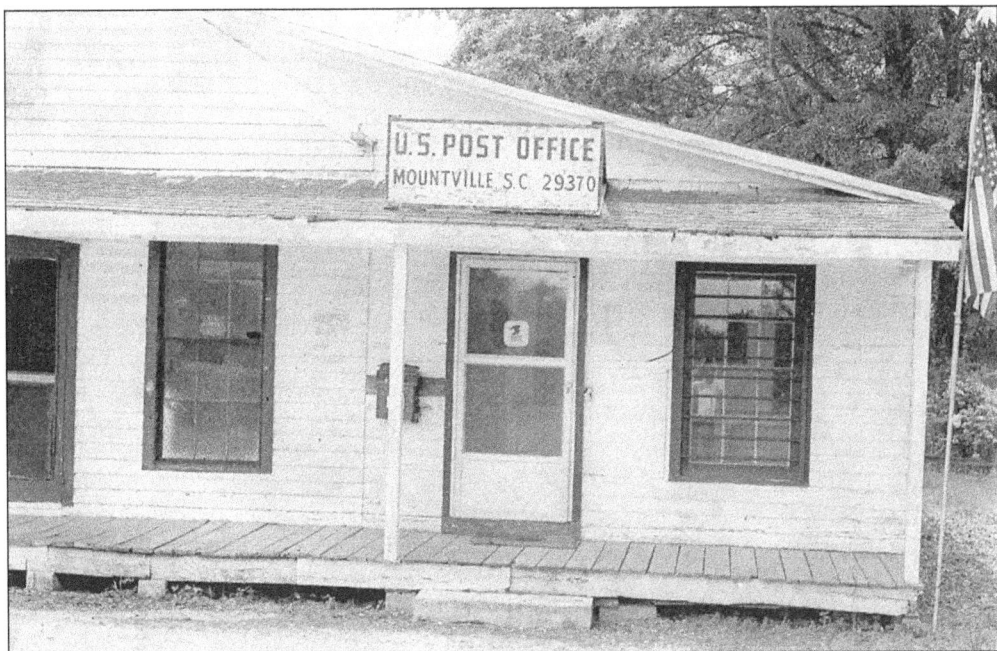

MOUNTVILLE POST OFFICE. In 1892, the Seaboard Railroad was completed through a section of Laurens County that became known as Mountville. A town suddenly appeared, and houses, churches, a school, a bank, and post office were constructed. (Courtesy Rhodes Collection.)

BENJAMIN REUNION. Members of the Benjamin family gather at Beaverdam Baptist Church for a family reunion. Benjamin family members were active in the early Baptist church, as well as in the Mountville community. The old church in the background was organized in 1807 with 59 members. Shortly before the War between the States, a brick building was constructed to serve the congregation, and clay for the brick came from local farmers. (Courtesy Mrs. Myrna Benjamin Self.)

OCTOGENARIAN. John Young Benjamin spent a long and active life as a farmer in the Beaverdam section of the county. Since his early adulthood, Benjamin was a member and deacon of Beaverdam Baptist Church. He was first married to Fannie May Benjamin and, of that union, came 12 sons and daughters. He and his second wife, Betty Knight, had one daughter. Betty was originally affiliated with the Chestnut Ridge Church. John died at the age of 80 at the Benjamin homeplace. (Courtesy Mrs. Dora Benjamin McMahan.)

BEAVERDAM FARMER. William Silas Benjamin (b. 1853) was married to Sara Francis "Fannie" Chandler of the same community. They were the parents of five children. Apart from being a farmer, Benjamin was active in community affairs as well as the Beaverdam Baptist Church. (Courtesy Mrs. Dora Benjamin McMahan.)

104

SOUTHERN BELLES. Eula Irene Benjamin, the daughter of John Young Benjamin and Fannie Elisa Carlton May, married John Shell Benjamin, the son of William Silas » and Sara Frances "Fannie" Chandler Benjamin. John Shell was a carpenter and farmer, and the couple had four children: Dora Bell, Henry, Margaret, and Fannie Mae. Eula Irene Benjamin is remembered for her love of gardening and her skill as a seamstress. She is pictured here with family friend Mae Stone. (Courtesy Mrs. Dora Benjamin McMahan.)

COUNTRY GENTLEMAN. Henry Lee Benjamin is portrayed here as a country gentleman, c. 1940, in the yard of the century-old Benjamin house in the Beaverdam community of Hunter Township. Henry was a textile employee and later became a brick mason. He is the son of the late Eula Irene and John Shell Benjamin. (Courtesy Mrs. Dora Benjamin McMahan.)

GOLDVILLE MANUFACTURING. James S. Blalock and his son L.W.C. Blalock built a small yarn mill in the Goldville section of the county. The post office in the area was originally called Huntsville, then Martin's Depot, and later Goldville because James Blalock purchased the property with gold. After a period of non-profitable operations, the company, which was originally called Goldville Manufacturing, was sold and became known as Banna Manufacturing. The textile mill later became known as Joanna Cotton Mills after the wife of a one-time owner. (Courtesy Laurens County Library.)

PASLAY PLANTATION. This six-room house of early colonial design was built in 1784 by Capt. Robert Paslay, who served in the Revolutionary War under Gen. Francis Marion. Originally the property extended from Beaverdam to Mountville, and Paslay probably obtained it in payment for services rendered during the Revolution. Paslay and his wife are buried in the family burial ground near the house. (Courtesy Cecil Milam.)

CAPTAIN PASLAY. Edmund Taylor Paslay was the son of Capt. Robert Paslay and he continued to operate the family plantation after his father's death. Paslay was zealous in organizing militia units and was, therefore, also known as "Captain" to his friends and neighbors. He lived in his family's home filled with heirlooms that included a corner cupboard, a Chippendale secretary, highboy, lowboy, wine table, and rosewood and mahogany piano. (Courtesy Cecil Milam.)

LISBON PRESBYTERIAN CHURCH. Located six miles south of Laurens, this church was organized on May 20, 1871, and Rev. Zelotes Holmes was its first pastor. In 1884, the church had 46 members. (Courtesy Laurens County Library.)

NICKELS-MILAM HOUSE. This three-story frame structure, constructed *c.* 1828 by Dr. John Nickels in the Lisbon community, is a variation on Greek-revival architecture. The family of Dr. Nickels was instrumental in founding the Lisbon Presbyterian Church. Charles L. Milam, a farmer and politician, purchased the property in 1920, and it has remained in the Milam family since that time. (Courtesy Cecil Milam.)

FARMER, CHURCHMAN, POLITICIAN. Charles Llewellyn Milam, born in 1879, was the son of Robert Barlett and Sybilla Paslay Milam. He and his wife, the former Mary Eleazer of Irmo, were the parents of six children. Milam purchased the John Nickels house in the Lisbon community, where he lived with his family; they were members of the Lisbon Presbyterian Church. Milam served in the South Carolina State House of Representatives for 18 years, placing great emphasis on better business and sound government. He was also a prosperous farmer. (Courtesy Cecil Milam.)

Seven

CROSS HILL

DR. JOHN HENRY MILLER HOUSE. Dr. John Henry Miller constructed this house c. 1880. Born in 1857 to Mary and Henry Miller, the physician married Liela Black, and after her death, married Liela's sister Ella. Dr. Miller was a well-known and respected Cross Hill physician and a member of Liberty Springs Presbyterian Church. He was a descendant of the McGowan family that settled in the Cross Hill area after emigrating from County Antrim, Ireland in 1801. (Courtesy Rhodes Collection.)

LIBERTY SPRINGS. This church was organized in 1787 under the leadership of the Rev. John McCosh, and after his death, the church almost vanished. In 1796, a few families petitioned the Presbytery of South Carolina for a ministerial supply, and Rev. J.B. Kennedy answered the call to serve the congregation made up of Irish immigrants. The first funds for the restoration of Mount Vernon came from the congregation to which Ann Pamela Cunningham's family belonged. (Courtesy Rhodes Collection.)

CROSS HILL METHODIST CHURCH. In the early years, Cross Hill had a Methodist church, but with the passing of time and the lack of an adequate congregation, the small, framed Methodist church was forced to close its doors. In later years, the building became a Masonic hall. (Courtesy of Rhodes Collection.)

CROSS HILL STORES. Located near the railroad, this line of small business establishments once served the thriving little town of Cross Hill. For many years, Weldon Leamon operated a general merchandise store in one of the buildings. At one time, there were approximately 20 stores and 5 doctors in the town of Cross Hill. (Courtesy Rhodes Collection.)

STORE PROPRIETOR. Miller Leaman is shown inside the caged office of Leaman Brothers Store in Cross Hill. The Cross Hill native was a respected businessman and member of Liberty Springs Presbyterian Church. (Courtesy Rhodes Collection.)

111

EARLY CROSS HILL HOME.
Mrs. Sara Copeland once
owned this home located on
Main Street in Cross Hill.
Members of the Watts and
Ball families have inhabited
the house at different times
through the years. (Courtesy
Laurens County Library.)

DIAL HOME. Located in
Cross Hill, the white two-
story house was the residence
of Miss Eleanor Dial. Dial
was born in 1900 and had
a long and successful career
as a church worker and
schoolteacher. She taught
the men's Bible class in 1921
at Poplar Springs Baptist
Church near Ware Shoals,
a rare opportunity for a
woman in that day. (Courtesy
Rhodes Collection.)

WOMEN'S RIGHTS PIONEER. Dr. Anne Austin Young of Cross Hill was the second daughter of Robert Alexander and Clara Nabers Austin. A Presbyterian College graduate, she was among the leaders who endeavored to establish the first state institution for the mentally handicapped that is today known as the Whitten Center. Young married a surgeon in 1918 and joined his practice as a gynecologist-obstetrician and the only qualified psychiatrist in the upstate. (Courtesy Rhodes Collection.)

MYRTLE WARD CROWDER. The daughter of Susan Coats Ward and John Ward, Myrtle was born on the Ward farm, south of Cross Hill. This 1914 photograph was taken just prior to her marriage to Clayton Crowder, the son of John Crowder. After the couple's marriage, the Crowders resided near the Milton section of Laurens County. (Courtesy James Julian Coats Jr.)

113

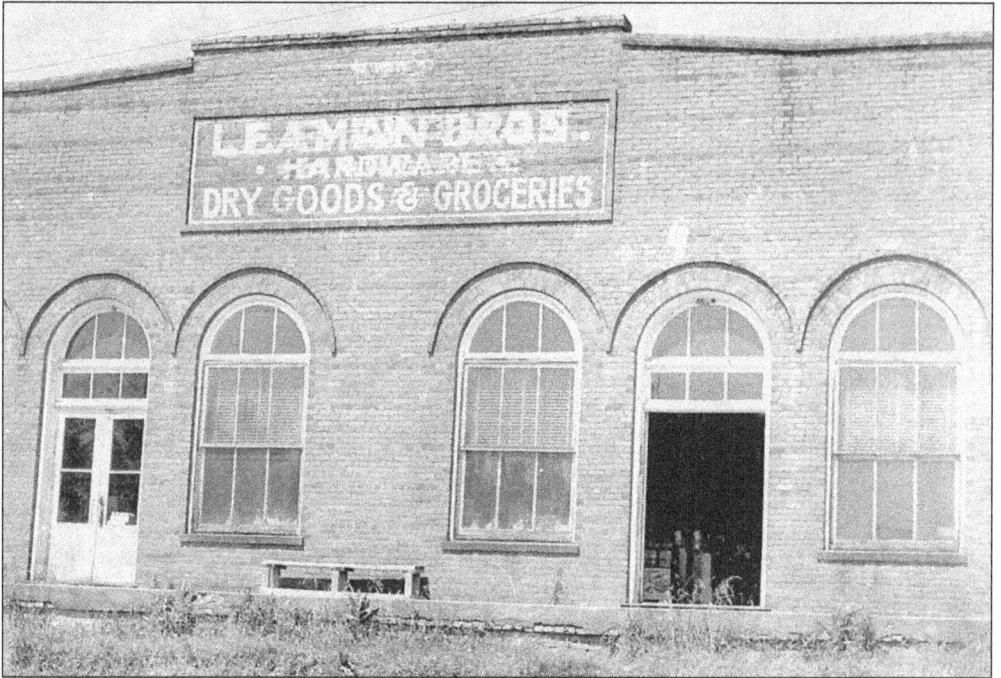

MILLER LEAMAN. J.E. Leaman opened a general merchandise store in Cross Hill in 1912 and operated it until 1931. Miller Leaman came into the business with his father in 1927. In 1931, Miller and his brother Sam ran the store and changed the name to Leaman Brothers General Merchandise. The slogan of the store was "If we don't have it, you don't need it." (Courtesy Rhodes Collection.)

CROSS HILL GENTLEMEN. These three young gentlemen were born in the Cross Hill section of Laurens County and were cousins. From left to right are Will Crowder, James J. Coats, and Jim Crowder. (Courtesy James Julian Coats Jr.)

BROTHERS AND SISTER. Robert VanDorn Coats (b. 1861) and Lydia Dora Hazel Coats (b. 1868) were residents of the Cross Hill area and the parents of four sons and one daughter. Pictured, from left to right, are the Coats children: Gilliam, Robert, Eva, James, and Wallace. The family moved to Laurens in the early 1900s. (Courtesy Rhodes Collection.)

SPORTSMEN. Wallace (left) and Robert H. Coats, the sons of Robert VanDorn and Lydia Hazel Coats, moved to Laurens shortly after 1900. Even though the brothers left the country and the farm behind, they never lost their passion for rabbit and quail hunting. (Courtesy James Julian Coats Jr.)

115

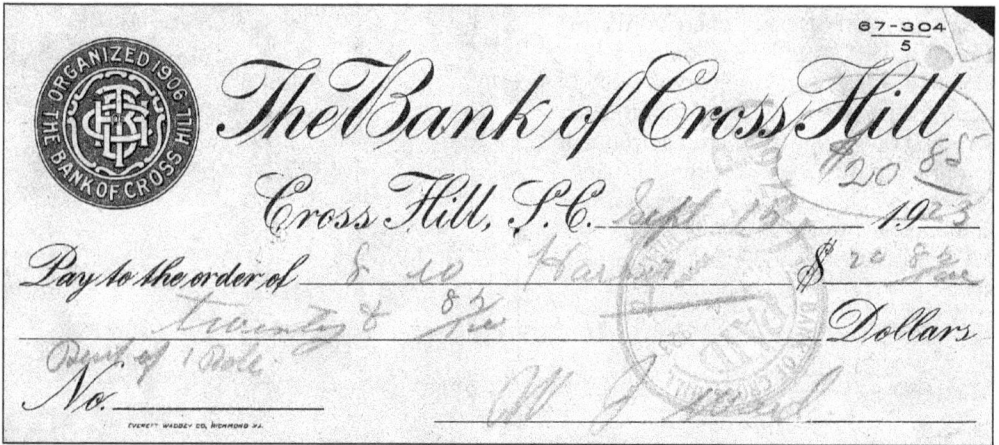

BANK OF CROSS HILL. Once a booming little country town, Cross Hill boasted a bank, as well as numerous general merchandise stores, several doctors, a milliner shop, and a depot. (Courtesy Rhodes Collection.)

KOON-DENDY PLACE. The builder of what became known as the old Koon-Dendy Place is unknown. The two-story house that was once surrounded by farm buildings rests on Highway 39 between Laurens and Cross Hill. (Courtesy of Rhodes Collection.)

Eight

JACKS

T.W. WIER HOUSE. Dr. Thomas Withrow Wier Jr., the son of Dr. Thomas and Nancy Long Wier, followed in his father's footsteps as a physician and planter. After marrying Lou L. Buchanan in 1879, Dr. Wier Jr. and his family settled in the Renno community and were active members Duncan's Creek Presbyterian Church. Shown in front of the old home are, from left to right, Mrs. Lou B. Weir, Lou Ralston, Sam Lawrence, Dr. Wier Jr., Caldwell Wardlaw, Withrow Long, George Robert, and Thomas Preston. George Buchanan is sitting on the porch. (Courtesy Mrs. Elizabeth Roper Miller.)

OLD WIER HOME. Born in 1800, Dr. Thomas Withrow Wier Sr., the son of Thomas and Mary Withrow Wier, was of Scotch-Irish descent. After completing medical college, he settled near Duncan's Creek Presbyterian Church and became an active elder. He married Nancy Long, the daughter of Robert Long, a soldier in the Revolutionary War, and the couple reared eight children. Dr. Weir was a signer of the South Carolina Ordinance of Secession. (Courtesy Robert H. Roper III.)

COPELAND FAMILY. The family of Benjamin F. and Annie Davidson Copeland has its roots in the Duncan Creek section of eastern Laurens County. The Copelands arrived in Laurens County prior to the Revolutionary War. Elizabeth Copeland Weir; her husband, Caldwell (in the bowtie); and their children, C.W. Weir Jr. and Virginia Weir; and other family members appear in this photograph. (Courtesy Robert H. Roper III.)

HURRICANE SCHOOL. A school was established between 1880 and 1890 for the educational needs of children in the Hurricane community. Teachers worked for low pay and often in undesirable conditions. This photograph of Hurricane School was taken in 1911. (Courtesy Laurens County Library.)

OLDEST CHURCH IN LAURENS COUNTY. As early as 1752 a settlement arose around the junction of Duncan Creek and the Enoree River, and John Duncan, a Scotch-Irish pioneer from Pennsylvania, was the first settler. Twelve years later, the Duncan Creek Presbyterian Church was organized and a primitive log structure was constructed. The present church was built c. 1842 and is one of the earliest examples of rural church architecture in upper South Carolina. (Courtesy James L. Cooper Jr. Collection.)

RENNO CLASSROOM. Between 1880 and 1915 many school buildings were constructed in Laurens County, especially in the smaller communities and rural areas. The Renno School was constructed in 1912. (Courtesy Laurens County Library.)

STANDS EMPTY. Renno was once a thriving little town in the Jacks Township of Laurens County and had doctors, a school, and stores. The train made regular stops in the little town. The remaining store now stands empty. (Courtesy Rhodes Collection.)

Nine

YOUNGS

WALLACE PLANTATION. Even though a bachelor, William Wilkerson Wallace built this house in 1845, and at the housewarming, he met and fell in love with Arianna Cheshire of Atlanta, who returned in 1846 as his bride. Surrounding the house were edifices that included barns, a blacksmith and carriage shop, a well house, a servant's house, a smoke house, and stables. Standing in the yard of the historic house, c. 1893, are Arianna and two of her six children, Mary Allen and Susan Elizabeth Wallace. (Courtesy Miss Stella Owings Wallace.)

WALLACE PLANTATION YARD. Standing in the yard of the Wallace Plantation House are Stella Owings Wallace, the wife of Allen Watson Wallace, and her young daughter Stella. Also pictured is Watson "Watt" Wallace with a dog. The plantation house and original fence can be seen in the background. (Courtesy Miss Stella Owings Wallace.)

AN ELOQUENT SPEAKER. After attending Wallace Lodge School, Columbus Rhett "Pet" Wallace attended Reidville and Cokesbury Colleges. Known as an eloquent speaker and writer, he served as the Sunday school superintendent of Bramlett Church, was appointed postmaster at Young's Store, and served two terms in the South Carolina State House of Representatives. Born in 1856 to Ariana and William Wilkerson Wallace, Pet became the owner of Wallace Plantation after his father's death. (Courtesy Miss Stella Owings Wallace.)

WALLACE HOMEPLACE. Located on Beaverdam Creek Road in Young's Township, this house was believed to have been constructed by Watt Wallace in the late 1800s. Pictured in the front yard of the homeplace are, from left to right, Ariana, Jessie, Mattie, Watt, Allie, Jennie, and Wilk Wallace. (Courtesy Miss Stella Owings Wallace.)

YOUNG'S COUPLE. Watt Wilkerson Wallace was the son of William Wilkerson Wallace, the original owner of Wallace Plantation built in 1845. Born in 1852, Watt was married to Mattie Llewelly Kelly in 1877. (Courtesy Miss Stella Owings Wallace.)

Owner of Wallace Plantation. Born in 1879, William Wilkeson "Wilk" Wallace was married to Elizabeth Mae Wharton, and the couple lived in the Wallace Plantation House. Wilk owned the plantation until his death, at which time it was inherited by his daughter Ruth Wallace Cheshire. Allen Watson Wallace later purchased the property for his daughter Stella Owings Wallace. (Courtesy Miss Stella Owings Wallace.)

Wallace Family. Sitting for a photograph, c. 1909, are members of the William Wilkerson Wallace family. From left to right are (front row) twins Ruth and Ralph, Allen, and Nell; (back row) Wilk, Earl, and Mae Wallace. (Courtesy Miss Stella Owings Wallace.)

Dr. Wil Lou Gray. Wil Lou was the daughter of William Lafayette and Sarah Lou Dial Gray. A graduate of Columbia College, she completed graduate work at Winthrop, Vanderbilt, and Columbia Universities. Wil Lou began her teaching career at Jones School in 1903 and then moved to Wallace Lodge, where she began the first adult education classes in Laurens County in 1915 while serving as the supervisor of rural schools. (Courtesy Laurens County Library.)

Laurens Builder. Kemper Bascom Brownlee, born in 1892, was the son of Mary Etta and James T. Brownlee of the Youngs section of Laurens County. He was married to Cathryn Hollis of the same community, and they were the parents of five children. Brownlee was well known for his draftmanship and carpentry skills and is credited with constructing more than 50 houses in Laurens County, as well as the Army barracks on Sullivans Island. (Courtesy Charles E. Hellams Jr.)

HOLLIS FAMILY. Mrs. Kate B. Hollis and her children pose for a photographer in front of the Hollis family home, located on the border of the Scuffletown and Youngs Townships. Standing, from left to right, are Mrs. Hollis and her children, Eva Hollis Miller, Margaret Hollis Burns, Charlie Hollis, Alice Ruth Hollis Porth, and Cathryn Hollis Brownlee. (Courtesy Charles E. Hellams Jr.)

CHEEK BROTHERS. Henry, James, Walter, Warren, and Spears Cheek, the sons of Willis Cheek, congregate for a Cheek family reunion. The Cheek family was well known in the Dials and Youngs Townships. (Courtesy Mrs. Sarah Alice Curry Limehouse.)

GOLD STAR MOTHER. Rosa Cannon and Will Rhodes lived in the Friendship Baptist Church community before moving to Laurens. They were the parents of twelve children. Two of their sons, Robert and Allen, were killed during World War II, and later, the Laurens Chapter of the Gold Star Mothers was named in their mother's honor. (Courtesy Rhodes Collection.)

BROTHER AND SISTER. Gladys and Willis Rhodes were born in the Friendship Baptist Church area of Laurens and were the youngest of the 12 children born to Will and Rosa Cannon Rhodes. The family later moved to the town of Laurens. (Courtesy Rhodes Collection.)

ACKNOWLEDGMENTS

We are deeply grateful to the citizens of Laurens County for providing information and lending photographs for this book. As we traveled throughout the county we met many new and interesting people. They opened their doors wide and entertained us with family and community stories as we turned pages of photo albums and sorted through treasured photo boxes.

Telling the story of Laurens County in these few pages proved to be an impossible task. Perhaps at a later date we can create another book to honor more of the truly great men and women of Laurens County.

To Elaine Martin of the Laurens County Library we wish to express our appreciation for use of materials in the library's South Carolina Room Collection, and for once again sharing her knowledge of Laurens County.

To friends Sarah Jane Armstrong and Eddie Hellams, thank you for locating and identifying photographs, for "burning the midnight oil" with us, and for all that you do to keep our county's history alive.

To Jim Brown, owner and publisher of the *Laurens County Advertiser*, thank you for allowing us to use back issues of the newspaper to verify historical data.

To Laura Daniels and the Arcadia staff, we wish to offer a sincere thank you for your advice and patience during the publishing of *Laurens County*.

Lastly, we would like to thank our families for their encouragement, constant support, and also for sharing memories.

Meeting new people and learning more about Laurens County has been a rewarding experience for us. What is more, it has been great fun.

FARMALL TRACTOR. During the 1930s, tractors began replacing mules on Laurens County farms since using a tractor was faster than plowing with a single-blade plow. (Courtesy James L. Cooper Jr. Collection.)

128